Paul Celan

A Biography of His Youth

THE BUKOVINA

= 80 km (48 mi.)

Paul Celan

A Biography of His Youth

ISRAEL CHALFEN

TRANSLATED BY MAXIMILIAN BLEYLEBEN

INTRODUCTION BY JOHN FELSTINER

PERSEA BOOKS

NEW YORK

In memory of

Moshe, Yuval, and Rosa.

First published in English in the United States by Persea Books in
1991, by arrangement with Insel Verlag. Originally published
by Insel Verlag as *Paul Celan: Eine Biographie seiner
Jugend* by Israel Chalfen, copyright © 1979 Insel Verlag.

Library of Congress Cataloging-in-Publication Data

Chalfen, Israel, 1909–
    [Paul Celan. English]
    Paul Celan : a biography of his youth / Israel Chalfen ;
    translated by Maximilian Bleyleben ; introduction by John Felstiner.
        p.   cm.
    Translation of: Paul Celan : eine Biographie seiner Jugend.
    Includes bibliographical references and index.
    ISBN 0-89255-162-3 : $22.50
    1. Celan, Paul—Biography—Youth.   2. Poets, German—20th century—
Biography.   I. Title.
PT2605.E4Z5913   1991
831'.914—dc20
[B]
                                                            91-25855
                                                               CIP

Designed by Vincent Torre
Set in Electra by Keystrokes, Lenox, Massachusetts
Printed and bound by Haddon Craftsmen, Scranton, Pennsylvania

First U. S. Edition

For we, which now behold these present days,
Have eyes to wonder, but lack tongues to praise.

Selbst uns hier heut,
den Zeugen deiner Gegenwart:
ein Aug, das staunt,
kein Mund, der preist, gegeben ward.

—from Shakespeare's *Sonnet CVI*,
German by Paul Celan.

CONTENTS

PREFACE

I owe the idea of writing a biography of the young Paul Celan to an early friend of his, Ruth Lackner, who wishes here to be referred to by her maiden name. I hesitated for a long time and asked myself whether it would not be too much of a risk to attempt a biographical work, even if intended to represent only the poet's early years, so soon after his death.

Two motives, however, led me to start work on the project in the fall of 1971. One was Celan's work itself, which I was convinced could only be understood with a knowledge of his biographical background. The other motive was the opportunity, which I could not see recurring in the future, of collecting information and documentary material.

Celan's poetry has occupied me intensely since I first encountered it in the late 1950s, and yet certain elements of it have remained dark and incomprehensible even after years of reading. When I met Celan in Paris in 1961, I asked him to interpret one of his poems. His answer was soft-spoken and melodious: "Read! Just keep reading. Understanding comes of itself."

I followed Celan's advice and did not stop reading. I also read the many interpretations, presentations and critiques of his poetry, which were being published even during the poet's lifetime and have multiplied since his death. The variety of views and often opposing interpretations sometimes do more to confuse the reader than to contribute to an understanding of the poetry. And if, lastly, one arrives at Beda Allemann's sentence, "We are confronted with the far from easy task of only just developing the criteria that would make possible a well-prepared approach to the second . . . half of Celan's lyrical work,"[1] then the reader finds himself alone and has to remain content, for the time being, with a purely subjective appreciation of the poems.

As a fellow countryman of Celan's, I seemed to find much greater meaning in the biographical element than is generally assumed. I felt, even before I knew it, that much in Celan's poetry refers to his childhood and youth in the Bukovina, to his native home which has remained an "unknown landscape" to today's reader. Hans-Georg Gadamer seemed to have had a similar impression when he wrote, "Perhaps some of Celan's poems will only be revealed to us when we have received more information . . ., from the knowledge of friends, from the results of purposeful inquiries."[2]

Paul Celan divulged only sparse information about his youth. Concerning his childhood, in the real sense of the word, he never revealed a thing. What is known until now is best summarized by Beda Allemann's "Biographical Data" in the two-volume collection of poems which he edited for Suhrkamp. Surely Celan's biographical evidence also includes remarks he made in the course of his acceptance speeches in Bremen and Darmstadt.[3] And certainly one can add to this his joking ironic response to a survey.[4] All this, however, constitutes a rather meager yield.

Celan told his later friends nothing of the early years in his native region. This is why Jerry Glenn, who had hoped for information from Celan's Viennese friends for his complete presentation of the poet's work, began his introduction with the observation that, "Practically no information regarding Celan's family or early years is available."[5]

Nonetheless, quite a few relatives, friends, and acquaint-

Preface

ances who survived world war, ghetto, and dispersion remember the young poet. Above all, Ruth Lackner needs to be mentioned. She owns a dedicated manuscript of his early poetry as well as some personal letters. She guided me by collecting the first addresses of relatives and friends from his youth, which then allowed me to seek out more witnesses. All those questioned received me with helpful openness and a willingness to make existing documents available to me. Their kindness was touching at times. Celan's aunt in London, Berta Antschel, answered my questions with trembling hands, while the others I approached provided me with the names and addresses of further acquaintances. The information I gathered in this way hooked up like the links of a chain. Finally, the leads provided by more than fifty interviewees and correspondents helped build the basis for the work at hand.

I express heartfelt thanks to all those who through selfless collaboration—be it in discussions and letters or in the willing surrender of documents and photographs—made possible the completion of this biography. Most of all, however, I thank Ruth Lackner, who suggested this idea and continually inspired its development. I owe thanks to Beda Allemann for encouraging me to bring the commenced biography to its end. Recognition is also due to Hermann Meier-Cronemeyer, who examined every page of my manuscript with friendly, critical eyes. And Stefan Reichert deserves exceptional recognition for the tremendous sympathy and meticulousness which gave the final shape to this manuscript.

Israel Chalfen
Jerusalem, summer, 1978

ACKNOWLEDGMENTS

This biography is based on information about Paul Celan that was passed on to the author in letters and conversations. The author produced written reports of each of the relevant conversations. When the source of a quotation in the text is attributed to a conversation, then it is to be understood that these are reconstructions based on the written notes. The dates on which the letters were written, or on which the interviews took place, are recorded in the back of this book in the alphabetized Index of Sources, an index of persons who gave information about Celan.

Poems that were published in the volumes from *Mohn und Gedächtnis* to *Schneepart* are cited from the two volumes of collected poetry:

> Paul Celan: *Gedichte in zwei Bänden*. Mit einem editorischen Nachwort von Beda Allemann. (Frankfurt: Suhrkamp, 1975).

The notes referring to Celan's poems appear in shortened form. The title of the poem is followed, in parenthesis, by the name of the volume in which it first appeared, and then by a Roman numeral indicating the volume of the collected works (I or II) and the corresponding pagination, i.e.:

> "Oben, geräuschlos" (Above, soundless) *(Sprachgitter)* I, 188.

•

Acknowledgments

The works collected in the two volumes first appeared on the following dates by the indicated publishers:
Deutsche Verlags-Anstalt, Stuttgart:
    1952 *Mohn und Gedächtnis*
    1955 *Von Schwelle zu Schwelle*
S. Fischer, Frankfurt:
    1959 *Sprachgitter*
    1963 *Die Niemandsrose*
Suhrkamp, Frankfurt:
    1967 *Atemwende*
    1968 *Fadensonnen*
    1970 *Lichtzwang*
    1971 *Schneepart*

Celan's first volume of poetry, *Der Sand aus den Urnen*, was published in Vienna by A. Sexl, 1948.

Earlier poems were quoted from three handwritten or typed collections, described in chapters V and X. They are referred to here as TS 44, MS 44/45, and TS 57. These collections, as well as Celan's Romanian lyrical and prose poems, are now published in *Das Frühwerk* (Frankfurt: Suhrkamp, 1989).

Following are the notes to the poems that head each chapter of this book:

The Shakespeare quotation is from the following edition: William Shakespeare: *Einundzwanzig Sonette*. Deutsch von Paul Celan. Mit einem Nachwort von Helmut Viebrock. (Twenty-one Sonnets. German by Paul Celan. With an epilogue by Helmut Viebrock.) (Frankfurt: Insel, 1975), p. 39. The English from: *The Complete Works of*

Acknowledgments

William Shakespeare (New York: Avenel, 1975), p. 1208.

Ch. I: from "Hervorgedunkelt" (Darkened Forth) *(Schneepart)* II, 367.
Ch. II: from "Ins Nebelhorn" (Into the Foghorn) *(Mohn und Gedächtnis)* I, 47; Hamburger, p. 65.
Ch. III: from "Drüben" (Over There), *Der Sand aus den Urnen*, p. 5.
Ch. IV: from "Blume" (Flower) *(Sprachgitter)* I, 164; Hamburger, p. 115.
Ch. V: from "Flimmerbaum" (Shimmering Tree) (Die Niemandsrose) I, 233.
Ch. VI: from "Erinnerung an Frankreich" (Memory of France) *(Mohn und Gedächtnis)* I, 28; Hamburger, p. 51.
Ch. VII: from "Und mit dem Buch aus Tarussa" (And with the Book from Tarussa) *(Die Niemandsrose)* I, 289.
Ch. VIII: from "Sternenlied" (Stars' Song), MS 44/45.
Ch. IX: from "Flügelnacht" (Night of Wings) *(Von Schwelle zu Schwelle)* I, 128.
Ch. X: from "Schibboleth" (Shibboleth) *(Von Schwelle zu Schwelle)* I, 131; Hamburger, p. 97.

TRANSLATOR'S NOTE

Unless otherwise indicated, all English versions of Celan's poems are by the translator. Translations by Michael Hamburger are from *Poems of Paul Celan* (New York: Persea, 1988), copyright © 1988 by Michael Hamburger, reprinted by permission of Persea Books.

INTRODUCTION

That the practice of biography is richly flourishing nowadays may seem paradoxical, when current literary theory would have us consulting or unraveling texts, not authors. And given the many recent studies of Paul Celan's writing that focus solely on its rhetorical or philosophical aspects—how negativity operates, how Heidegger pertains—it might seem impertinent to seek out the personal background of those enigmatically compelling poems. Celan himself was extremely reticent about his early years, and if asked about the meaning of a poem, he habitually replied (as Israel Chalfen tells us): "Read! Just keep reading. Understanding comes of itself."

Yet there is good cause, and a specific need, for bringing into focus the early life of this poet, even though in 1945, at the onset of his career, there was nothing left to him but the German mother tongue: only language, he said, only "this one thing remained in the midst of the losses." In fact, precisely because he lost family, culture, and the Bukovina homeland, that loss itself came to ground his writing.

When Paul Celan was born in 1920, Bukovina had just become a small province of northern Romania, and Czernowitz, his birthplace, was only recently the eastern outpost of the Austro-Hungarian empire. Nearly half the city's population were Jews, many of whom staffed the economy and professions as well as various Zionist and non-Zionist organizations. At the same time, Celan's childhood coincided with the loss of liberal Austrian hegemony and the rise of Romania's Iron Guard and fascist anti-Semitism, which ranged from virulent to violent. By his mid-teens, students in Romania were at risk for Communist or Socialist tendencies, and after 1933, Jews were gradually even more at risk.

Yet like millions of others in central and eastern Europe, Celan's family persistently saw their destiny there rather than in emigration. He himself survived forced labor camps during the war years, but his parents did not. When northern Bukovina passed to the Soviet Union at war's end, Celan had nowhere to dwell but within the German mother tongue, memory-rich and memory-ridden. While this poet invested so much, absolutely, in the language of his poems, nonetheless nearly every poem he wrote derives from some specific datum—a place, person, event, coincidence, phrase, citation. Chalfen's biography of Paul Celan's early years gives substance to the loss the poetry attests.

Certainly we do "keep reading," and the growing spate of critical attention suggests that Celan's poetry is still approaching a peak of interest in America, England, Europe, and Israel. Suhrkamp (who published the German paperback of Chalfen's biography) is gradually issuing an elaborate "historical-critical edition" of all Celan's work; meanwhile Jerry Glenn's superb bibliography lists over 3000 items through 1989, and the flow has continued apace.

The subtitle of Chalfen's biography, *Eine Biographie seiner Jugend*, will ring a bell for those familiar with Klaus Wagenbach's biography of Kafka's youth. Indeed Celan felt a lifelong kinship with Franz Kafka, leaning toward traditional Judaism yet at odds with both Orthodox spirituality and Jewish assimilation. Unfortunately we lack from Celan—he never could have brought himself to compose—anything like Kafka's *Letter to His Father* (1919) or Osip Mandelshtam's *The Noise of Time* (1925), retrospections on their middle-class Jewish upbringing.

Introduction

Both men figured sharply as tutelary spirits for Celan. Shortly after the war he translated four of Kafka's stories into Romanian, and later he worked intensively for six months making his German versions of Mandelshtam's poems. "Rarely have I had, as with his poetry," Celan said, "the sense of making my way alongside the Irrefutable and the True."

Kafka and Mandelshtam were true writers also touching Celan's fate as a Jew. He once told a friend that Kafka's *Letter* had to be written over and over again in Jewish homes. Yet despite the distancing from his father that troubled Celan, his own recovery of childhood would not have exhibited Kafka's or Mandelshtam's ambivalence tinged with disgust at the loose ends of Central European Jewish assimilation.

The reason for this difference is stark and simple to state. As distinct from Kafka, for Celan something drastic intervened before his maturity: a chasm split open between his youth and any recollective memory of that youth. Nazism virtually effaced his pre-war childhood, along with the Czernowitz social and cultural milieu that Chalfen describes. The precious little we know from Celan's own mouth comes as oblique, fragmentary glimpses in his conversations, letters, lectures, and occasional prose. Chalfen has assembled a firsthand account from numerous interviews, memoirs, and other documentary sources. But in a sense, the true substance of that obliterated childhood appears irretrievably lost—except as perceived through the diffracting medium of poetry.

The vital source at the heart of that childhood, as at the heart of its irretrievable loss, is the boy's mother Friederike or Fritzi, deported to Transnistria and murdered during the winter of 1942. "This word is your mother's ward," the poet tells himself in a 1951 lyric; and a later poem addresses her as "your being-dead's daughter," thus summoning a mother arrested in

Introduction

time, uncannily becoming as young as her offspring. There exists a striking photograph showing Paul Celan's mother at about twenty-one, with full soft features and warm gaze under a very large felt hat, her hand in a suede glove resting on a book. On the back of the photo he has written, "Mama, during the First World War, in Bohemia." The handwriting, along with that word "First," date from after the next war, the war from which his mother could not find refuge.

What the wrenching overnight loss of his parents actually did to him, or whether the murder of his mother at German hands made this poet dwell more precariously within his mother tongue, we can only infer and speculate. Chalfen sketches in the mother's beloved presence through various reminiscences by friends from Celan's youth. One of these, a fellow student in 1940 when the Russians had occupied Czernowitz, told Chalfen: "I remember a whole series of colorful sweaters and vests into which his mother's caring hands had knitted beauty and love." But she also says, "No close friend knew very much about his inner life."

Paul Celan's primary loss, the primary event we may most wish to know more about, when his parents were abruptly rounded up and deported, still remains somewhat obscure. Celan himself never gave a full account, that I know of. According to Chalfen's source, Ruth Lackner, she had found her friend Paul and his family a small factory office to stay in over the Saturday night when roundups were occurring. Paul's mother took a fatalistic view, and he argued with her. But his parents did not follow him into hiding. Returning home after the weekend, he found the front door sealed, his mother and father gone.

This version of Celan's sunderance from his parents at the age of twenty-one does sound likely enough, and traumatic enough to have somehow conditioned everything he wrote until his death—a suicide by drowning in 1970. Yet other versions exist of what happened that fateful night. Although not altering essentially the blank fact of sudden loss, they attach slightly different circumstances to it, thus coloring differently Celan's lifelong sense of having crucially abandoned his parents.

It may be that Chalfen's paramount reliance on the testimony of Ruth Lackner for much of his biography should ideally have been modified by other witnesses. Several Bukovinians who knew Celan before and after the war have thought so. And perhaps Israel Chalfen's own inclinations led to a more Jewishly oriented image of Celan than might have resulted from another biographer using other informants.

To be sure, Celan was no Elie Wiesel, who stemmed from a Hasidic ambience with Yiddish and Hebrew on the tip of his tongue. But neither was he a Primo Levi, with a wholly secular and assimilated upbringing. I think Chalfen's material bears out the half-traditional, half-assimilated existence that Nazi and Romanian anti-Semitism struck so jarringly, so irrecoverably. In any case, a number of brief and disparate reports concerning Celan's life have emerged since Chalfen wrote his pathbreaking biography, whose interviews occurred mostly in the early 1970s, soon after Celan died. There is indeed room, as always, to develop further the picture of his youth, and the poet's latter career still remains to be chronicled.

An account of his early years is of the essence, as Celan himself implied on more than one occasion. His much-studied speech "The Meridian," accepting the 1960 Büchner Prize, constitutes a brilliant *ars poetica* for literature under historical crisis. At the close of this speech, Celan says that at bottom he has been seeking "the place of my own origin. I am seeking all that with an unsure because restless finger on the map—on

Introduction

a children's map, as I readily admit." Whatever reality his pre-war childhood took on for Celan's imagination, it did so because unnatural, rupturing loss entered in. How far this is from our Romantic vision!—from Coleridge's pregnant remark, "Genius is childhood recovered at will." And how far from our portraits of the artist as a young man à la James Joyce or Dylan Thomas.

A biography of his youth must inevitably embed Paul Celan in the German-Jewish cultural matrix of Bukovina, and will seem to fix the poet's identity that way. But other identifications have been asserted, and they matter decisively in the war's aftermath of conflicting cultural politics. Celan has been a figure that stirred much debate, partly owing to certain aspects of his career: the obsessional notoriety this Jew's great elegy "Todesfuge" ("Death Fugue") generated in postwar Germany; an unfounded plagiarism charge-cum-campaign against him; his suicide; and of course the unprecedented quality of his poems. Because of such things, Celan has for many years been a problematic and prized figure, at times a contested commodity.

Many claims for his identity are in the air, some more valid than others, and all testifying to a complex, migrant destiny. His two years in Bucharest (1945–1947) give him a Romanian dimension; his 1948 sojourn in Vienna and his family's Habsburg Empire origins have enabled some people to actually call him an Austrian writer; his perfect French, his mature decades in Paris, and his marriage to the artist Gisèle de Lestrange made for a many-faceted connection to France, though the country never embraced him; his frequent trips to Germany and regular publication there make it easy to label him a German poet; his long-deferred visit to Jerusalem and Tel Aviv in 1969, welcomed fervently by the German-speaking community,

Introduction

and some lyrics he wrote immediately thereafter, tightened a link to Israel; his youthful leanings toward socialism, solidarity with Republican Spain, mystical tendencies, affinity with certain literary and philosophical doctrines, have each gained him adherents and a titular status.

Could one of these elements alone identify Paul Celan? He was above all a poet—perforce and often by choice a Jewish poet, so uncompromising that any other definition seems partial. Chalfen's pages amply bear out the two interpenetrating destinies of poet and Jew.

This book also locates in Celan's youth the beginnings of a genius that has increasingly come to be valued and evaluated—namely, his verse translations from various languages. Here you can follow, up until age twenty, the gestation of a linguistic facility that seems extraordinary even in the post-Empire, polyglot, history-ridden milieu of central Europe. French he had a penchant for from his early teens, developed it into a fluency that astonished his schoolmates, and eventually translated twenty-three poets from Baudelaire on. English came more slowly, but we're told that even in the Czernowitz ghetto in 1941 Paul was reciting Shakespeare and translating sonnets. Later he made brilliant, idiosyncratic versions of Emily Dickinson and others. Russian, when Soviet troops occupied Bukovina in 1940, became a useful, employable skill, then again under the 1944 occupation, and during the fifties Celan's fascination drew him to Esenin, Blok, and particularly Mandelshtam, whom he translated as a blood brother.

Meanwhile Romanian, absorbed thoroughly by Celan in the state schooling of his childhood, stayed with him closely enough so that just after the war he wrote some poems in that second language, and translated Russian prose and drama for a Bucharest publisher. Finally Hebrew, which he studied intensively but then dropped after his Bar Mitzvah in 1933, percolated back to him in the aftermath of Nazi oppression. Although he translated only a few pieces from one Israeli poet, key Hebrew terms and German wordplays upon Hebrew turn up in highly revealing ways throughout Celan's own work, including the first word of a famous Bialik lyric he must have memorized as a child in Hebrew school.

The reminiscences Chalfen has gathered also document Paul Celan's early literary enthusiasms, most of which eventually became influences. He reportedly loved to recite Rilke to his friends, and his first girlfriend remembers him at age sixteen as having "something of Hölderlin's prophetic gift." It seems richly coincidental that the great poets he prized when he was young, Rilke and Hölderlin, should now be those with whom Celan's own name is aligned when commentators designate the high order of German poetry.

Another welcome resource provided by this book emerges where Chalfen cites early lyrics by Celan. Most of these are available only in recent scholarly editions, and very few of them have been translated into English before. Often the attachment of these poems to a place and time illuminates both the verse and its biographical situation. What is more, Celan's nineteen months in forced labor camps away from home gave rise to scores of poems, composed as if in counterpoise against the discomposure of loneliness and shoveling rocks. Celan was bound to Ruth Lackner during this period, and many expressive passages from letters he sent her accompanying his newly-written poems appear here for the first time.

Sometimes, however, Chalfen sounds to me too literalistic in attaching a poem to a certain situation; but this seems a minor hazard of biography. What's more puzzling is why he does not discuss "Todesfuge"—though he does quote a touch-

Introduction

ing letter about it from the older poet Rose Ausländer. Evidently written in Czernowitz in late 1944 or early 1945 and published two years later in Bucharest, this poem belongs within the frame of Chalfen's narrative. In fact, some of his most valuable material feeds directly into an understanding of the poem's emotional sources: namely, the personal reports that Chalfen gathered from survivors of the camps where Celan worked, and of the Ukrainian stone quarry to which his parents and compatriots were deported.

Schwarze Milch or "Black milk of daybreak we drink it at dusk," the shocking opening of "Todesfuge," and the poem's quotable refrain, "Death is a master from Germany," still provide the well known (and perhaps too well assimilated) signal of Celan's achievement, especially in Germany. Already by the early 1960s, Celan felt that this great lyric was becoming a kind of "reparations" poem in German mouths, whereas his writing had by then turned away from readily accessible metaphor and idiom.

Yet "Todesfuge" and its striking catch phrases continue to mark Celan's prominence. German highschoolers for two generations have chanted and analyzed the poem out of countless textbooks; on the 50th anniversary of Kristallnacht in 1988, it was recited in the Bundestag; and recently German television entitled a major Holocaust documentary *Der Tod ist ein Meister aus Deutschland*.

But beyond all this, Celan's voice, line by line etching away at silence in his mother tongue that had "passed through the thousand darknesses of deathbringing speech," as he put it—Celan's voice speaks through poems that have cut deep into consciousness and conscience, in Europe, America, and elsewhere in the world. We may see and hear ourselves in him.

To our misfortune and ironically to our gain, the suicides

Introduction

of Celan, Jerzy Kosinski, Primo Levi, and lesser-known writers
such as Jean Améry and Piotr Rawicz, make us listen attentively
to voices changed utterly by the war in the middle of this
century.

> No one
> witnesses for the
> witness,

Paul Celan once wrote. His own poems along with Israel Chalfen's biography help redeem that silence.

John Felstiner
Stanford, California, 1991

I

The Unknown Landscape

HERVORGEDUNKELT, noch einmal,
kommt deine Rede
zum vorgeschatteten Blatt-Trieb
der Buche

DARKENED FORTH, once more,
comes your speech
to the shadow cast ahead
of the beech's leaf-shoot.

F ROM the crest of the Carpathian Mountains steep slopes
fall eastward into wide valleys. The mountain range runs across
low hill country into the Prut River plain. This region is home
to rich vegetation: the bristling underbrush of mountain pine
grows above the timber line, dense woods of spruce cover the
middle heights, and forests of beech-trees spread over the lower
regions. The beech gave the landscape its name. Slavs and
Romanians call the tree "buc." German and Austrian attempts
to change the name of the Bukovina into "Buchenland" (beech-
land) were never successful. The higher regions are sparsely
inhabited, but the closer one comes to the Prut and to Czernowitz, the only large city of the region, the denser the network
of villages, market towns, and small cities becomes.

"The landscape from which I come to you," Paul Celan

Paul Celan

said in 1958 at his acceptance of the Bremen Literature Prize, "is likely to be unknown to most of you." A few lines on, he specified that ". . . it was a region inhabited by people and books," and spoke of "this former province of the Habsburg Monarchy now a victim of historylessness."[6]

The Habsburgs had occupied the Bukovina with its many peoples in 1774. Here lived Ukrainians, Romanians, Jews, Germans, Poles, Magyars, Hutsuls,* Lipovanians,† Slovaks, Czechs, Armenians, and Gypsies. Although Ukrainians comprised only a third of the country's population, they formed the majority in the northern plain between the Dniester and Prut rivers. The Romanians, who only migrated into the Bukovina from Transylvania over the Carpathian passes as late as the twelfth century, settled mainly in the mountainous South and constituted another third of the entire population. Since German builders, workers, and businessmen were already here in the Middle Ages, the Habsburgs settled the newly acquired lands with colonists from different regions of Germany and the Habsburg Monarchy. The German minority made up barely nine percent of the population. Each of the other ethnic groups made up no more than three percent—with one exception: the Jews, of whom there were twelve in every hundred inhabitants.[7]

It was in fact the little-respected Jews who helped the Habsburgs succeed in establishing a German stronghold in the eastern part of the monarchy. Jews had been living in this region, which had formerly belonged in part to Poland, in part to Moldavia, since the thirteenth century. Following their expulsion from German lands at the time, the Jews had been

*A Ukrainian-speaking tribe of mountaineers and herders, said to be descendants of the Dacians who fled from the Romans into the forest. —M.B.
†Immigrant Russian "Old Believers" of a sect founded by Philipp, a Russian Orthodox monk. —M.B.

4

admitted by the region's ruling princes, who were favorably disposed toward them. In the course of time they prospered as merchants and businessmen. But the frequent Russo-Turkish wars of the eighteenth century, which also adversely affected parts of Poland, brought about economic crises and anti-Semitic attacks in Russia and Poland. Many Jews were compelled to flee into Moldavia, which was less involved in the war, and whose northern region was later named "Bukovina" under Austrian rule.

At first, the Austrian military administration wanted completely to "do away with" the Jewish refugees who had settled in Czernowitz, but Joseph II prevented their expulsion based on his "intention to make of the Jews useful members of the State." As a result, plans were drawn up to bring "the Jews to the cultivation of land by distributing them among the lords of manors," as well as to make "good traders or workers" out of them.[8] And the imperial intention bore fruit: in the course of nearly 150 years of Austrian rule, admirable farmers and numerous high-quality craftsmen were to be found among the Jews. It was not until the years 1941 and 1942, when the Jews were driven out by German Nazis, that these conditions of relative peace and security came to a gruesome end.

Even as subjects of the Moldavian rulers, the Jews enjoyed religious freedom as well as autonomy in community and educational affairs. When the Austrians disputed these rights, the Jews resisted tenaciously and wrested the privileges back from their new rulers. But sharp disagreements over religious matters also flared up within their own ranks. Around the middle of the eighteenth century, the orthodox rabbinical tradition of East European Jews was split as a result of the popular movement of reform Hasidism. Orthodox rabbis considered this movement heresy and attacked it tirelessly.

Paul Celan

In the year 1841, the Hasidic zaddik, Israel Friedman, who had fled his Ukrainian hometown of Rischin, made the Bukovina his second home.[9] He built his "court" on the former property of a Russian general in Sadagora, next to Czernowitz. It soon became a place of pilgrimage, although the "Haskalah"—the Jewish Enlightenment movement—increasingly challenged Hasidism as well as Jewish orthodoxy. The Viennese regime of 1815–1848, which was very concerned with clericalism and obscurantism, supported the rule of the Zaddik of Sadagora against the Haskalah, which transmitted modern European knowledge and education to the Jews in Hebrew.

The short-lived success of the Viennese revolts of 1848 did not yet grant the Jews civil rights. Their position was strengthened, however, by the administrative reforms of the next year, in which the Bukovina was separated from Galicia and elevated to a crownland. Here the Jews, together with the Germans, constituted one third of the population. While most of the other inhabitants remained loyal to their Ukrainian or Romanian mother tongues, German became the native language of the Jews, who were finally emancipated in 1867.

The Jews' equal status also put an end to the inter-Jewish struggle against the Enlightenment. Although Hasidism remained meaningful within small circles of Jews until the end of the Second World War, the residence of the Zaddik of Sadagora, already destroyed by the Russians in the First World War, became the ruined symbol of this movement's inevitable decline.

Even today, the former Jewish inhabitants of the Bukovina remember the nearly half-century-long period between the Emancipation and the First World War—the last decades under Habsburg rule—as the "Golden Age." Although anti-Semitism grew in Vienna and in the Austrian traditional provinces of the Habsburg empire, it was hardly noticeable in the Bukovina, where the Jews formed a counterweight to the irredentist efforts of Slavs and Romanians. In Austrian patriotism, the Jews even outdid many Germans, who, as members of the pan-German movement, tended to wave black, red, and gold flags rather than black and yellow ones.

The active cultural life of the Bukovina was deeply indebted to the Jews for important influences. They were the most eager visitors and patrons of the Czernowitz City Theater, which featured Viennese guest performances in addition to plays by its own ensembles. In the musical realm as well, supporters were mainly Jews. They backed the orchestra of the music society, for example, and supported the National Museum of History and Art of the Bukovina.

Around the turn of the century, Jews constituted one third of all students at the German Franz-Joseph University, founded in 1875, and Jewish university professors were no longer a rarity in the city.

Three independent German language daily newspapers and several magazines were edited by Jewish journalists. Several Jewish poets and German language writers received recognition even beyond national boundaries. In this way, Karl Emil Franzos's stories *Aus Halb-Asien* were widely read in Germany; Leo Ebermann saw his drama *Die Athenerin* premiered in the Vienna Burgtheater; Erich Singer published his *Bukowinaer Musenalmanach* in Leipzig; the young lyrical poet Kamillo Lauer received the 1909 Hofmannsthal Prize in Vienna; the poet Viktor Wittner wrote and published his poems and theater critiques in Vienna and became chief editor of Berlin's *Querschnitt* in the twenties.

German-Jewish poets were also active during the Bukovina's Romanian era, and publications in German written and published by Jews appeared in Czernowitz until 1940. The literary magazine *Nerv*, founded in 1919 by the German-Bukovinian poet Albert Maurüber, although very popular among young Jewish poets, soon folded. Overall, the German poetry of Bukovinian Jews remained entirely unrelated to that of Germans at home or in Transylvania. Those poets who sought literary support turned instead to the schools of poetry that existed in the German literature of Central Europe.

Jewish intellectuals were able to befriend Romanian and Ukrainian intellectuals most easily if they had attended the same German language schools and universities in the Austrian days. Writers, journalists, and artists who were united by the German language often met at the "Schwarze Adler" or at the "Café Europe." These conversations also resulted in invitations of German theater-ensembles, including even the Yiddish "Wilnaer Truppe" from Lithuania. Art exhibits of local Jewish painters and sculptors, such as Kolnik or Löwendal, attracted Jews as well as non-Jews. National Romanian cultural agencies, however, only provided support to Romanian artists.

Although Jews were very quickly assimilated into German culture, as in all German-speaking areas, they protected their Jewish heritage and tradition to an even greater degree than elsewhere. In fact, they developed a novel sort of pragmatism that permitted them to be modern while retaining from Judaism the elements that gave their lives moral support and allowed them to safeguard their ethnic identity. No liberal Judaism emerged, and the self-denying assimilation, that was widespread in the German lands of the monarchy, reached at most a small section of the upper class that spent most of the year in Vienna.

The economy profited considerably from the emancipation of the Jews. They became landowners, or administered the extensive, wooded property of the Greek Orthodox Church Foundation, giving timber export a strong impetus, just as Jewish agronomists contributed greatly to the modernization of agriculture. And with the rise of industrialization, many Jews built and managed the steam-powered sawmills, the distilleries and breweries, the sugar factories, and the cement, glass, and textile plants, either alone or with non-Jewish financiers. By the beginning of the twentieth century, Jewish industrialists, businessmen, and bankers were a leading force in the economic life of the crown-land.

In the First World War, Jewish soldiers and officers were more patriotic than Ukrainians and Romanians, since they saw in the Dual Monarchy the guarantor of their freedom. They knew they had everything to lose and nothing to gain. And when the land became a battlefield, the Jews fled from the Tsar's notorious Cossacks deep into the monarchy, while it was hardly rare for Ukrainians and Romanians to welcome the Russian invasion.

When, during the collapse of the Habsburg Monarchy in 1918, Romanian troops advanced on the mutinous Austro-Hungarian troops, all the ethnic groups in the Bukovina claimed minority rights. They created national assemblies and handed over their demands to the peace conference that convened in St. Germain. The Jews also mobilized their American friends to garner additional public support. The talks dragged on for months because the Romanians, who had been promised the Bukovina, persistently refused to accept the stipulated minority rights. An ultimatum from the great powers and a change of government in Romania finally made the signing of a peace treaty possible. This occurred in 1920, the year of Paul Celan's birth.

But the Romanians did not take the enforcement of these

Paul Celan

minority rights particularly seriously. They were much more concerned with transforming the Bukovina as quickly as possible into a Romanian province—to "Romanize" it. Above all, they worked to remove the Jews from all the prominent positions they had held under Austrian rule. In order to comply at least partially with the obligations they had agreed to, they allowed the various nationalities to operate schools in their respective languages. Since the Jews, divided among themselves, demanded Yiddish as well as Hebrew schools, the Romanians decided upon German-language instruction for Jewish students with Yiddish and Hebrew as elective courses. However, before the Jews were able to resolve the language conflict among themselves, the Romanians quietly transformed all the minority institutions into Romanian schools in the late 1920s. Later, only private schools were permitted to choose the language of instruction according to their own judgment. All student candidates, however, had to pass their graduation exam (Abitur) in Romanian. The language question was in this context only one aspect of the ideological disunity of the Jewish post-war generation in the East.

Three ideologies arose in the mid-thirties in response to the Jewish question, which was growing more acute under Romanian rule: Zionism, territorialism, and socialism. Assimilation into the Romanian national culture offered the Jews of the Bukovina nothing. Even the Zionists, who argued in favor of instruction in Hebrew and emigration to Palestine, spoke German at their conventions and published the *Ostjüdische Zeitung* in German. In the first decade after the war, Zionism became the strongest political movement among Bukovinian Jews, but by the thirties it had already begun to lose much of its popularity. The territorialists fought for the preservation of Yiddish and the autonomy of Jews in the countries of the Diaspora.

The Unknown Landscape

Socialism attracted many Jewish intellectuals, but its appeal was of a more Zionist or territorial nature than a social-democratic one. The Romanian Social Democracy was under strong internal political pressure. The Communist Party was outlawed. Nevertheless, communism won the sympathy of many young Jews in the thirties.

At the end of the First World War, the Bukovina's economy was depressed. Destruction at the hands of the enemy and shortages of raw materials had paralyzed industry and severely curtailed trade. The Jews, as inhabitants of the cities, felt the effects of the economic decline more severely than the rural population. The Romanian government could help little, and its investments profited almost exclusively those citizens of Romanian origin. American-Jewish relief funds had to be established, and years passed before the crisis was overcome. Although another prosperous Jewish bourgeoisie became established in the thirties, it never reached the significance it had held in the Austro-Hungarian empire.

Between the two world wars, the Jews of the Bukovina fought tirelessly for their civil rights and the maintenance of their traditional way of life. Whatever the constitution of the Romanian parliamentary kingdom offered them was fully exploited. They created a Jewish-national party, which was able, together with the Jews of all Romanian provinces, to dispatch its representatives to the Bucharest parliament. Jewish candidates were successful in some district council elections. For over two decades (1918–1940), the Romanians in Czernowitz had to tolerate the thriving Jewish life which resisted all anti-Semitic attacks. A quiet, but tenacious fight for Jewish self-assertion was in progress.

The Jews of the Bukovina remained loyal to their German mother tongue even under Romanian rule. The older generation either did not learn Romanian at all, or only as much as was necessary to deal with the authorities. The young had to learn the state language in school, but few of them developed a personal, intimate relationship with it. The Jews had seen the downfall of a world in the collapse of the Habsburg Monarchy. But among them, the Austrian tradition survived.

"That which was within reach, distant enough, but still to be reached, was called Vienna," Paul Celan said in his acceptance speech for the Bremen Prize.[10] Students in the Bukovina preferred Austrian universities. When the Romanians introduced policies restricting entry for Jews at the medical faculties, studying in Vienna became almost a necessity.

"It was a region inhabited by people and books," to use Celan's words again.[11] The bookshops, which belonged primarily to Jews, offered the latest, most important publications from Vienna, Berlin, and Leipzig. The most successful Jewish bookseller in Czernowitz, Josef Bernfeld, was a Doctor of Philosophy and a scholar. Decades later, the former bookseller and Paul Celan would meet, both in exile, in Paris.[12]

Personal and social contacts between Christians and Jews, which dated from the Austrian era, remained intact under Romanian rule. However, there was very little contact between Jews and those Romanians who settled there after the First World War. From the early Austrian era, Jews and Christians were accustomed to visiting one another on Sundays and holidays. In a special tradition the Christians would invite Jews to their Christmas celebrations and the Jews would reciprocate for Purim, the Jewish carnival. In a land dominated by the Greek Orthodox church, the Catholic carnival was not celebrated publicly, so the equivalent Jewish festivity attracted even more interest.

Officially, Czernowitz was a provincial city of Romania;

in reality, however, it had to be seen as a German-language Jewish city. Roughly 50,000 Jewish inhabitants in a total population of 110,000 formed its character. The Jews lived dispersed throughout the entire city, but in the center the business signs were nearly all engraved with Jewish names. Shops, offices, legal and medical practices were owned by Jewish craftsmen, businessmen, lawyers, and doctors. From bankers and representatives of independent professions to tailors and barbers—all were Jews. Everywhere in the city one could hear their Bukovinian German, with its Austrian informality and Slavic breadth, and interwoven with Yiddish idioms. Here, the words borrowed from Yiddish gave their colloquial German color and warmth, and gave rise to a sort of dialect which had never, in the true sense of the word, been formed in the Bukovina. At this meeting point of Eastern and Central Europe, life was raucous and lively.

Plains and hill-country meet at the northern entrance to the city. From the valley of the Prut one can see the hill on which the city lies. Its cliffs rise steeply above the neighboring towns of Kaliczanka and Klokuczka, which lie in the river valley. The hill was divided by the main entrance road, whose twists and turns formed segments with different names: Brückenstrasse, Bahnhofstrasse, and Hauptstrasse. The western slope was covered with the green parks of the Habsburgshöhe, the private park of the Göbelshöhe and the Schiller municipal park. Only on the hill's eastern face is the slope gentler. The road, however, had not been developed much to the East, and the suburb of Horecza on the eastern shore of the river lies far from the city center.

If one crossed the large stone bridge over the Prut and climbed into one of the red and white cars of the single electric tram line in the city, one soon reached the main train station

Paul Celan

of the National Railroads, whose domed roof and glass hall recalled Vienna. One continued with the *Elektrischen* up the steep gradient of the main street and wondered how the small streetcar could reach the top of the slope. The steepest part was even called "das Schief" (the slant). Alongside the tram, horse-drawn carts and light carriages were also driven—motorcars were still a rarity—and the tram "conductor" had to ring his bell vehemently to warn the pedestrians who crossed the tracks as they wished and also to drown the yelling coachmen and the cracking of their whips.

The Ringplatz was the heart of the city. Here traffic lights already existed, but hardly anyone heeded them. The sidewalks were always overcrowded with passers-by who were in no hurry. They strolled along in a leisurely manner, and when someone ran into an acquaintance both stood still, even in the heaviest crush, to chat for a while. "Nur mit der Ruhe!" ("All in due time") was the motto here.

The tram continued south up a much lighter incline, through the Rathausstrasse, past the bulky *Magistrat*—the town hall with its square clock tower—into the Siebenbürgerstrasse which extended far into the distance. Next came the Romanian cathedral with its round tower and the unadorned high school next door. On the opposite side of the street, between the chestnut trees, one could see the former provincial government building, which slightly resembled a neoclassical temple. The small Franz-Joseph square, with its green space, looked like the large building's frontyard. The drive then continued along the wide Volksgarten, before reaching its final destination at the southern train station. At this point the surroundings had a very rural appearance: vegetable gardens alternated with sports fields, and the railroad tracks stretched between them. A gravel path, flanked by free-standing wooden houses, led into the fields of the surrounding area: the Flurgasse, a popular walking trail. On the outskirts of the city, one found country wells in open courtyards:

Erzähl von den Brunnen, erzähl
von Brunnenkranz, Brunnenrad, von
Brunnenstuben—erzähl.

Tell of the wells, tell
of the well-wreath, well-wheel, of
well-rooms—tell us.[13]

To one side of the busy Siebenbürgerstrasse, between the municipal building, police headquarters, and the pseudo-Gothic Catholic Herz-Jesu Church, lay a spacious terrain, taken up in part by a public garden and in part by the timber market. The new residential area of the Masarykgasse—one of young Paul Celan's neighborhoods—was built on an empty space next to it, in the thirties. Just behind the Herz-Jesu Church, in the Stefan-Wolfgasse, in an old building, was the former Ukrainian high school, which was renamed in the thirties after Crown Prince Michael as a Romanian high school. It was there that Celan received his diploma.

From the Ringplatz, the Herrengasse, the most elegant street of the city with the spacious properties of the big landowners from the previous century, turned off toward the Southeast. When their lands were partially expropriated after the First World War, these landowners converted their town houses into apartments, and installed small shops. Between noon and one o'clock, people gathered here for the *Korso*, or promenade. Contrasting with elegant young ladies, the students of duelling fraternities walked by, wearing their traditional heraldic colors.

15

Paul Celan

In the thirties they still stood leaning against the houses, with colorful caps and armbands, or sauntered in small groups. Among them one could also find members of the Jewish-national student societies, who wore Hebrew names like Emuna and Zefira embroidered on their lapels.

In the Herrengasse stood the solemn "Deutsche Haus" with an ornate gable, painted black, white, and red, with a wood-paneled beer hall on the ground floor. The large, German Renaissance hall was, like similar houses, readily and cheaply rented out to public and private organizations for many different functions and events. In the twenties, on important holidays, when the Great Temple, the place of worship for the Jewish religious community, and the synagogues of the private prayer communities did not suffice, the Jews would hold their service here. In addition, the room was made available to the Yiddish "Wilnaer Truppe" for their performances. In the thirties, the swastika-emblazoned flag fluttered from the roof. In 1940, Hitler brought the Germans of the Bukovina "home to the Reich."

The equally elegant Maria-Theresiagasse turned off the Herrengasse and crossed the Josephgasse to the Wassilkogasse, where Paul Celan spent his childhood. The Joseph- and Wassilkogasse were avenues lined with old chestnut trees. On these quiet streets were also the homes of landowners who found themselves impoverished after the war and were forced to rent out their city properties.

The western parts of the city could be reached from the Ringplatz by the Tempelgasse, which led across the Tempelplatz to the large Jewish temple. The temple was built in the Moorish style with four towers which rose like minarets, and its roof was crowned with a copper dome. In the entrance hall was a marble plaque in honor of Franz Joseph I. The career of the singer Josef Schmidt, whose song "went around the world," began in the boys' choir of this temple.

Across from the temple, the Romanian palace of culture blocked the once open view of the adjacent "Jewish House." It stood, to the side of the delicate city theater with its curved ramp and neoclassical columns, on the spacious stone-tiled floor of the Theaterplatz. The Jewish House, built in pseudo-Baroque style, made a ponderous impression with its three floors, garret roof and the stone figures at the entrance, as if in petrified mourning. The small alley alongside the building bore the name of Heinrich Heine.

The Schiller memorial in front of the City Theater had to give way in 1918 to a statue of the Romanian national poet Mihai Eminescu. But the public garden lying behind the theater was still called "Schillerpark." From its highest point one could easily look over the western plain, in which the Swabian town of Rosch and the Cecina mountain stood out clearly. Jewish hikers who walked to the Cecina on Sundays had to expect rock-throwing Rosch youths.

Northwest of the city lay the university quarter, the archbishop's residence and the Habsburgshöhe. The Moorish-Byzantine residence of the Romanian-Orthodox archbishop was among the most beautiful buildings of the old monarchy. At that time, the three religious leaders of the country, Archbishop Repta, the Prelate Schmidt, and the Grand Rabbi Dr. Rosenfeld, formed a "clover-leaf" through their unifying friendship renowned throughout the city.[14] In the First World War, Archbishop Repta saved the Torah scrolls of the Jewish temple from the Cossacks. In the Second World War, no one would do this—and the temple went up in flames.

The upper, newer part of town was connected with the lower, older part from west to east by the Dreifaltigkeitsstrasse, on which the simple house of the Jewish Construction Craftsmen's Guild stood. In this unadorned room, Paul Celan's parents were married.

Further down the hill and toward the East, lay the old Jewish neighborhood. The old Moldavian cities had no Jewish ghettos, but the Jews settled where an old water well from Turkish times or later an artesian well assured them a steady water supply. The Judengasse kept its bumpy cobblestones, and in the Synagogengasse stood the old synagogue with its heavy, fortress-like walls.

Where the old Jewish quarter joined the city center stood the Hebrew elementary school Safah-Ivriah, which Paul Celan attended for three years, and the Toynbee-Halle, a national educational institution with a large library and reading room with an attached Jewish apprentices' hostel. The anglicist of Czernowitz University, Leon Kellner,[15] was the spiritual father of the Toynbee Hall, modeled on an English design.[16] The money for the construction and furnishing had been provided by a rich Jewish industrialist.

As a high school and a university student, Paul Celan read in this library all of Kellner's own works and everything that told of his activities as a teacher and a politician. In 1968 Celan wrote to a compatriot: "More than once I . . . quoted this name, when I tried . . . to identify that which . . . had no name, tried to discuss that which was . . . placelessness."[17]

In Czernowitz and in all of Romania, as growing anti-Semitism became visible, the Jews remained optimistic. The fate of German Jews after the rise of Hitler in 1933 certainly aroused feelings of solidarity among Bukovinian Jews—they helped those driven out of the Third Reich who had to return to their former homes, and gave to the relief funds for German Jews—but they were convinced that anti-Semitism could not become politically effective in Romania as it had in Germany. In addition, many also thought that National Socialism was on its last leg. They did not see the writing on the wall.

In 1941, one hundred years after the zaddik from Ukrainian Rischin had found a second home for himself and for Hasidism in Sadagora near Czernowitz, his great-grandchildren were destined to be expelled from that home. Rabbi Ahron and Rabbi Mordechai Friedman, leading their last faithful followers, Torah scrolls in their arms, set out on the painful path to the East, from which they would never return.

Thus ended the life of the "people and books" in a landscape which, for one-and-a-half centuries, had been home to a Jewish-German "symbiosis."

II

Speak My Name

Reicht euch das Dunkel,	Proffer yourselves the dark,
nennt meinen Namen,	speak my name,
führt mich vor ihn.	lead me to him.

T HE Antschels named their son, born on November 23, 1920, Paul. This was the name entered on his birth certificate. But they gave the son a second name: eight days after his birth, the newborn was accepted into the "Covenant of Abraham," and received the Hebrew name "Pessach" during the ceremony. Pessach had been the name of one of his ancestors, his father's maternal grandfather. The Hebrew name was only to be used on religious occasions and passed on orally.[18]

In the religious beliefs of Orthodox Jews, the Hebrew personal name represents the immortal soul and should thus be passed on from generation to generation. This is also the reason for the frequent recurrence of the names of patriarchs and prophets.

Pessach is the Hebrew name for the Jewish feast of the

Paul Celan

Passover. The word "Pessach" means 'to pass over' in the sense of 'letting something go, leaving something by the wayside,' and refers to the last of the ten plagues with which Jahweh afflicted the Egyptians so that they would allow the Jews to leave in freedom. This last plague meant death for the first-born of every Egyptian family. But so that the angel of death would spare Jewish households, the Jews were told on that night to smear the blood of a freshly slaughtered lamb on their doorposts. In this way the Pessach or Passover feast indicates the sparing of Jewish first-born as well as the departure of the Jews from Egypt.[19]

Paul was born under the sign of Sagittarius. But his family considered horoscopes to be un-Jewish and far-fetched. Only much later would a girl friend of his youth, who was born under the same sign, speak to the poet of the symbolism of Sagittarius, and Paul Celan would then write:

> . . . den harten
> Novembersternen gehorsam:
> . . .
> eine Sehne, von der
> deine Pfeilschrift schwirrt,
> Schütze.

> . . . obedient
> to the hard November stars:
> . . .
> a bowstring, from which
> your arrow-script whizzes,
> Archer.[20]

Paul's parents—Leo, in Hebrew or Yiddish Arje-Leib,

Antschel-Teitler and Friederike, in Yiddish Frejde, neé Schrager but called Fritzi—had been married in early 1920. Many relatives and a few friends attended the marriage ceremony in the hall of the Jewish Construction Craftsmen's Guild. After the wedding, because of the economic troubles of the time, the young couple moved in with Leo's family, where his bachelor room was assigned to them as both a living- and bedroom. It was also the room in which Paul was born.

In the modest three-room apartment at number 5 Wassil-kogasse, on the ground floor of the old apartment house, the newly married couple lived with Leo's father—his mother was already dead—and with two of Leo's younger and still single sisters, Regina and Minna. Fritzi got along well with her sisters-in-law, and the joint household was kept in the best of harmony. The girls befriended their brother's wife and were happy to let her lead them. When Fritzi was due to give birth, Minna and Regina took care of her. Fritzi had lost her mother in childhood. Her father had entered a new, in fact his third, marriage, and his wife had borne him another son, who was then eight years old. Fritzi's natural siblings, Blanca and Bruno, still lived with their father. Since Blanca worked and Fritzi's stepmother had to take care of her own household, neither was in a position to help her during the birth. For this reason, Leo's sister Berta came from Vienna.

Under a midwife's supervision, Paul's birth was a normal one. His mother's labor pains were fierce and in those times no one attempted to allay them. The baby was healthy and developed nicely, breast-fed by his mother.

Leo rarely spent much time at home during the day. As a broker in the timber trade, he usually conducted his business in cafés. He had taken on this work in 1918 at the suggestion of an old friend. When he returned to the Bukovina from the

disbanded Austrian army, he could not find work appropriate
to his education. Shortly before the war he had graduated from
the State School for Construction and Industry and received
a degree in structural and civil engineering. But nothing was
being built in Czernowitz. Directly following the war, the
economy of the Bukovina was depressed, and unemployment
was widespread. The population was almost exclusively dependent on local products such as corn meal and firewood. Corn
was the most widely-cultivated agricultural product and corn
meal had long been the most important foodstuff for the region's
inhabitants. The vast Carpathian forests provided firewood,
the only fuel for home or workshop. Many former businessmen
turned to the trade of these vital products. Leo, who had no
capital with which to open his own business, had to content
himself with work as a broker. After initial difficulties, he
managed, through diligence and honesty, to earn everyone's
confidence and become the permanent representative of major
timber trading companies. Although Leo's earnings were modest for a long time, he persevered in the work he had finally
obtained, which at least protected him and his family from
hunger. Nonetheless, it was two years—Leo meanwhile was
thirty—before he could marry Fritzi Schrager, to whom he
had been engaged before he left for the front.

Paul's parents came from Jewish families, some members
of which were long-time Bukovinians, while others had come
from eastern Galicia. His paternal ancestors had lived in the
Bukovina for generations while the maternal line had arrived
around the middle of the nineteenth century.

Leo Antschel-Teitler was born in 1890 in the village of
Schipenitz, north of Czernowitz, son of Wolf Teitler and
Chaje-Yente Antschel. His parents gave him a hyphenated
name because they, like many other orthodox Jews in those

years in the East, valued only the religious marriage ceremony and disregarded the registry office. Only once all of the children were born and, because they were considered illegitimate had received only their mother's family name, did the parents decide to fulfill the legal formalities. When the childrens' last name was corrected they were called in the old-Austrian official language "Antschel *recte* Teitler," and the hyphen was added only later. Over the years, all of Leo's siblings simplified their names: one brother chose the name Teitler, all the others, including Leo, decided on the maternal name—Antschel. When Paul became a student, he was initially called Antschel-Teitler, but once in high school simply Antschel.

Leo's parents gave him a strict orthodox education, which consisted mainly of studying the Holy Scriptures and the Talmud. He also attended the village's public German-language elementary school. Located in an Ukrainian region, the school also took into account this ethnic language. But the main emphasis of Leo's education remained on Judaism, which was the focus of Leo's father's life-long studies.

Leo's father, Wolf Teitler, had come from the neighboring village of Vassilev into the house of the prosperous Antschels in Schipenitz as a "learning stepson." This process was part of the Orthodox Jewish tradition. The small grocery shop, set up by his wife's parents so that they could earn a living, was run only by his wife.

The paternal line can be traced back another generation: Wolf Teitler was the son of Schikke (Yeshayahu) Teitler and Mathel Teitler, who lived in Vassilev. Schikke was probably a "Melamed," a teacher in the Hebrew school and the prayer leader of the village's small Jewish community.

Pessach Antschel, Chaje-Yente's father and Paul's great-grandfather, was reputed to be an industrious man, experienced in Jewish studies. He came to the Bukovina from eastern Galicia to begin a life of more practical work. This must have been the period after the Emancipation when Jews were permitted to own land, and the practical Antschel must have seen his future in farming. In his Galician homeland, the Jews were much less willing to make this "revolutionary" adjustment, and thus many young couples moved to the Bukovina to earn their living. Pessach Antschel bought a large farm, which he operated with the help of local laborers. He became affluent and gained the esteem of his fellow citizens. Christians and Jews came to him for advice, especially on agricultural matters. Pessach Antschel passed his property on to his daughters—he had no sons—and their descendants were landowners in the Bukovina until 1940.

By the turn of the century, the Enlightenment had penetrated every corner of the Bukovina. Even Wolf Teitler's children could no longer stand their parents' orthodox home. They wanted to take up active jobs and not to spend their lives with the sacred texts of Judaism. The first to leave the village was the oldest brother, David. He went to Germany and managed to become owner of a hardware factory in Schwarzenberg near Chemnitz. He was later driven from there by Hitler.

Leo Antschel-Teitler did not leave his parents' house until he was eighteen, and even then did not go very far. In Czernowitz, between 1908 and 1912, he attended the mid-level vocational school, which was then the German-language State School for Construction and Industry. When he received his final certificate he had to report for military service, as he had reached the age of conscription. The First World War broke out before the end of his compulsory service. Leo was first sent to the Russian, later to the Italian front. When wounded he was moved behind the lines to lighter service, where he remained until the collapse of the Habsburg Monarchy.

Speak My Name

Immediately following the end of the war, Leo rushed to Vienna to bring his father and sister home. Like most Bukovinian Jews, his parents and siblings had fled in 1916 into the interior of the monarchy, first to Moravia, where they found shelter in the village of Gaja near Brünn (later Brno). After the mother's death in 1917, they moved to Vienna where the oldest sister, Berta, there since 1914, worked in an office. Leo and his relatives returned home. They did not, however, want to return to their village and decided to settle in Czernowitz. Only Berta Antschel stayed in Vienna, and as the "Viennese aunt," she would play a significant role in Paul's childhood. In memory of his grandmother buried in Gaja, Paul Celan would one day dedicate to her "the pebble from / the Moravian basin," as it is a Jewish custom to place small stones on the graves of the deceased. [21]

In Czernowitz Leo saw his fiancée Fritzi again, whom he had only been able to visit on leave during the war. Fritzi was the daughter of the businessman Philipp-Schraga Schrager and his second wife, Adele Ehrlich, from Strozynetz in northern Bukovina. Fritzi had been born in 1895 in Sadagora, the same small Sadagora which, in the poem *Eine Gauner- und Ganovenweise* (A Tune of Rogues and Crooks), Celan calls the town near which the city of Czernowitz lies. According to a Czernowitz belief of unknown origin, the people of Sadagora were despised as rogues and crooks. [22]

Philipp Schrager had emigrated from eastern Galicia to the Bukovina toward the end of the previous century. He had tried his luck in several small provincial towns, and finally, after the death of Adele, his second wife and Fritzi's mother, he settled in Czernowitz. Adele had left him three young children of whom Fritzi was the oldest. He also had an adolescent son from his marriage to his first wife, who had died earlier. Fritzi, then twelve years old, took over the care of her younger siblings, four-year-old Blanca and two-year-old Bruno, and she fulfilled this task with dedication and responsibility. It was not until four years later that her father remarried. His third wife not only found healthy, well-developed children, but also, in her stepdaughter, an important help with her housekeeping.

As a result of the extraordinary demands made upon Fritzi in her younger years, her education suffered more than anything else. Aside from secondary school, which she could still attend regularly, she was only able to take one additional course in commerce. But whatever Fritzi did not learn in school she got from books. Very soon she displayed a taste for reading and spent every free moment with her books. She especially enjoyed reading the German classics, and in later years she would compete with her son Paul in quoting their favorite authors from memory. When her sister and brothers became older, she worked in a commercial office. Even during the war, she contributed to the family's income through her work as a children's nurse.

Fritzi's father was an Orthodox Jew. He often recalled his ancestors who were buried in Palestine—they had made their pilgrimage to the Holy Land long before—but nonetheless remained much more liberal than her father-in-law Teitler. Philipp Schrager followed the religious commandments, but made exterior concessions to the spirit of the times which Teitler did not permit himself. While, for example, Leo's father still followed tradition and wore the old-fashioned long caftan of the most devout and allowed his beard to grow unshaven, Fritzi's father dressed in the modern short jacket and was careful to display a meticulously cropped beard. He gave his children a worldly German-language education, transmitting to them from religion only what was of utmost necessity. But the youngest son, Esriel, borne by his third wife, had to attend the Yeshiva, the Talmud-school, on free afternoons in addition to junior high school because his mother, who came from a very devout home, demanded it. Nevertheless, Philipp was very proud of his son's successes in this field and rejoiced when Esriel was praised by the rabbi of the Yeshiva as his best student. Bruno, the son of his second marriage, wanted to become an actor, naturally to the grief of his father. He was only permitted to perform readings of German and Yiddish poetry. Later as an adult, he went to Paris where he found employment as a reciter.

Despite his appearance, which did not follow Jewish tradition, Philipp Schrager was patriarchal. Of middle stature, but broad-shouldered, he gave the impression of being a massive figure. He was a captivating conversationalist, and his intelligent remarks revealed extensive knowledge. As a businessman, he was obviously not very successful. His family's living standard was not much higher than that of the Teitler house.

During the First World War, the Schragers also fled from the Russian troops, but they went to Bohemia. First in Lubenz, then in Aussig on the river Elbe, Fritzi again took care of the household, since shortly before the hasty escape from Czernowitz her stepmother had gone to visit relatives in Galicia and was only later able to join her family in Bohemia. In one of Celan's poems, Bohemia will later appear as "your mother's three-year-land" and the Elbe in its Latin name, "Alba."[23]

Fritzi was a pretty woman. A photograph, with this remark on the back in Celan's handwriting: "Mama, during the First World War, in Bohemia," depicts a carefully dressed young woman with large, kind eyes. The evenly shaped face with its full, round cheeks still has something child-like about it, but her posture is clearly that of an adult. Unfortunately, the large

Paul Celan

fashionable hat hides her rich, blond hair, which is mentioned with admiration even today by her relatives. It is surely no coincidence of the photographic setting that her left hand is resting on a book in the picture, but is rather one of Fritzi's characteristic features.

When Leo met Fritzi, her life was rigidly aligned with the duties of the house and her work. She had few girlfriends and absolutely no male friends. Leo was an inexperienced youngster from the countryside, who had met Fritzi by chance in the company of his landlord's daughter and had immediately fallen in love with her. Whether Fritzi was also in love with the pleasant but unprepossessing youngster remains unclear. Some signs and later developments lead one to the assumption that Fritzi more likely expressed maternal feelings toward the lonely young man in the city.

The marriage of Leo and Fritzi appeared harmonious and happy to members of both families and to outsiders, but certain events lead one to suspect that both partners had to muster much self-control and understanding to sustain their marriage. Leo, who was able only after many years to grant his wife a certain degree of middle-class comfort, probably suffered all his life from guilt toward his wife, who, during the many years of living with his relatives, never had an easy life. This was probably why he made an effort, whenever he was able, to comply with his wife's wishes. Fritzi, on the other hand, considered herself solely responsible for the important decisions in the family, for she recognized her husband's insecurity and indecisiveness, which were also responsible for his difficulties in business.

As she was accustomed to running a household since childhood, Fritzi was a good housewife. Her sisters-in-law held jobs in the late twenties, and their means only rarely allowed them any domestic help. Still, her household always shone with cleanliness, and she could cook like no other. The couple had no social life; visits occurred only among relatives. Fritzi had a strong influence on the young and motherless girls in her family and that of her husband. She was a motherly friend, who always had advice. In later years, they called Fritzi "educator of an entire generation of the family."[24] All of them felt, and still feel, grateful to her.

Paul Celan's parents were at all times bound to the Jewish tradition. As typically pragmatic Bukovinians, they simplified their lives in such a way as to run no risk of breaking tradition too severely. Fritzi had learned this from her father and Leo from his life as a soldier. Of course, they showed consideration for Wolf Teitler's devoutness during the old man's lifetime. When he died in 1924, their lifestyle became even more liberal, but they remained believers and were loyal to the religious community. Every Friday night Fritzi lit the Sabbath candles, and the dietary laws were fully respected until 1940, when this became nearly impossible under Russian occupation. But they only went to the temple on major holidays, on Rosh Hashanah and Yom Kippur, because Leo had to work on Saturdays.

Leo's Zionist convictions were decisive in his attitude toward Judaism and Paul's education. To him, as to many other Zionists, Jewish tradition also meant a preparation for essential fulfillment, in other words, for the realization of the Zionist goal: emigration to Palestine. He doubted that he himself would be able to reach this goal, but was hopeful that his son would find a way there. When Leo's sister Minna moved to Palestine in the early thirties with her new husband, his hopes grew and he encouraged Paul to write to her in the Jewish homeland.

Paul Celan was an only child. The fact that he never had

brothers or sisters was clearly influential in his spiritual development. Thus he once said in his early years to a close female friend: "I want to be your brother; I have always wished for brothers and sisters." And the "sister" also plays a role in his early poetry. [25]

The Teitlers and the Antschels, the Schragers and the Ehrlichs, all passed a rich inheritance on to the future poet Paul Celan. The Teitlers transferred to him his Jewishness, the Antschels a love for nature, the Schragers and the Ehrlichs a devotion to the German language. The natural as well as the human landscape of his home was for the poet, throughout his life, the "land of wells," [26] which nourished his life and his work. After the Second World War he would write of the buried wells and their ashes. But the poet's recollections would then reach even further back: he would remember not only the catastrophe that struck his people, but also the dark row of ancestors who remained present in his spirit and his work.

III

Near You One Is Cramped

Den Wind hör ich in vielen Nächten wiederkehren:
"Bei mir flammt Ferne, bei dir ist es eng..."

In many nights I hear the wind return:
"For me distance burns, near you one is cramped..."

P AUL'S parents gave their son a conventional, middle-class education, in which Judaism served as a moral structure rather than as a religion. Jewish ethics were to shape his character and instill the behavior necessary for the social advancement they hoped for him. That his education had to be authoritarian seemed self-evident to them. His father, usually a very correct and compliant man, felt himself virtually obliged to impose his paternal authority to its full extent. He believed in the Jewish axiom that only the father who knows how to punish his son truly loves him. A close relative recounts:

Paul's father was a strict disciplinarian in his home. He was not a kind man. He was very demanding of his son, punished him, beat him often for every small, childish

37

offense. Leo was of a small build, almost a head shorter than his wife. You had the impression that he tried to compensate for his diminutive stature and failures in material life by being a tyrant at home. But he did not quarrel with his wife—he was very devoted to her. The son, however, received the brunt of the man's rule. Paul was a very sensitive child and suffered intensely from his father's severity. [27]

Although his mother also valued a strict education, she was able to express her maternal love through affection and consolation and to soften some of his father's more severe measures. His father, on the other hand, forbade everything which, in his eyes, would "spoil" the child. [28]

Young Paul learned early on to obey and behave in accordance with his parents' idea of a 'good upbringing.' He had to maintain painstaking physical hygiene, could not leave anything on his plate, nor could he ask any superfluous questions. But if Paul talked back or rebelled, or was childishly stubborn, he was heavily reprimanded by his father or even beaten. If Paul's 'offense' seemed particularly serious, his father locked him in an empty room and kept the key. Luckily, the room had a window leading to the backyard. The women of the house could thus free the bitterly crying boy as soon as the father had left the house for work. Usually his mother freed him, but sometimes one of his aunts did. During these incidents, Paul often had his own thoughts. Once, when his father had shouted, "What's to become of you, you rascal!?" Paul asked his cousin Klara: "What is a rascal? Something nice?"[29]

Paul spent the first years of his life almost exclusively in the company of adults. Aside from his parents, those who lived with them included his grandfather Teitler and his aunts Minna and Regina. Later his cousins Emma and Klara also joined them. His mother's sister, Aunt Blanca, was also often in the house.

His grandfather, old and sick, lived secluded in his room. Paul rarely saw him, but was repeatedly told not to make any noise, so as not to disturb him. Little Paul continually came up against limitations on his freedom: the doors which he could not open and the front door, through which he was only allowed to pass in the company of an adult. He was also forbidden to stay alone in the quiet Wassilkogasse, lined with chestnut trees. Sometimes, though rarely, he was given permission to play with the daughter, who was his age, of a music teacher living in the same house. And this was only allowed in the backyard, where a few trees and scanty grass grew. The wood supply for the winter, the fence, and the house door— these were the confines of the summer paradise of Paul's first three years of life. It is no coincidence that one poem from Celan's youth begins with the sentence: "Only beyond the chestnut trees lies the world."[30]

Paul must have been a "sad child," to use an expression from Rilke's *Book of Hours*. Child-like spontaneity was forced into propriety and his cheerfulness suppressed. A group photograph, taken in 1923 for the occasion of Aunt Blanca and her husband's departure for America, shows young Paul, barely three years old, sitting stiffly in front of his parents and looking sadly into the camera. His fingers are tensely intertwined in an odd way. Was Paul trying hard to imitate his grandfather who is sitting in the center of the picture with his hands clasped? The boy on the right side of the picture—a grandson of Schraga Schrager's first marriage—nestles fearfully by the old man's side, but seems almost more relaxed than Paul, who here seems compulsively rigid. This becomes particularly clear when one

39

compares Paul's posture to that of the third boy in the picture: eleven-year-old Esriel, Paul's step-uncle, who stands between his father Philipp-Schraga Schrager and his stepsister Blanca smiling self-confidently at the camera.

Paul's father looks straight ahead with an open, friendly expression. Paul's mother, on the other hand, seems worried and depressed. Despite her twenty-eight years, she already looks somewhat matronly. Just under four years of marriage and three years of motherhood have already strained the beauty of her youth.

In 1923, the year the photograph was taken, Aunt Regina also married and moved out of the family home. In the following year Grandfather Teitler died and left the room to his daughter Minna. She was temporarily without work and so followed the advice of distant relatives from the provinces. She took in their two daughters, who were to attend the girls' high school in Czernowitz. Klara and Emma Nagel from Milie in the northern Bukovina could not have been better taken care of than they were at Aunt Minna's.

But the two sisters also became Paul's best playmates and most intimate friends until he encountered children of his own age at kindergarten and at school. After completing their homework the two adolescents enjoyed playing with the little boy, since the adults rarely had time for Paul. It was not all play, however; most important were the fairy tales and stories which they told or read to him. If the book of Grimm Brothers' fairy tales, which Regina's husband had brought from Vienna, or the other children's books that Aunt Berta had sent from the same city, had been read often enough, then they turned to the Bukovina's extensive folklore to sustain Paul's happiness. Paul listened with rapt attention. He was soon able to retell every story. Finally the girls began inventing their own stories, and when Paul noticed this, he asked: "Did you write that?" It occurred to him that he too could "make up" fairy tales, and he began telling stories of his own.[31]

There was one person in the house who did not like the fairy tales. It was Paul's father, who considered the constant storytelling a waste of time. Leo Antschel wanted to raise his son as a sober man, not a dreamer. His opinion therefore was that if there must be stories, then they should at least be the educational ones from the Old Testament! But he hardly ever found time to tell them.

In his fifth year Paul entered the most exclusive and expensive kindergarten in the city, to which only the children of solid middle-class, mainly Jewish, families were accepted. The Meisler Kindergarten had maintained German as its language of instruction, while the Romanian language was little used. The choice of this kindergarten indicates the aims of Paul's parents. Their plans were ambitious and did not conform at all with the family's economically modest position. They considered no sacrifice too great for their son's expensive tuition. Paul was to enter the city's best social circles, keep his German mother tongue as pure as possible, take up an intellectual job, and live in honor and prosperity. They were also concerned with his Jewish education, especially his father, but in the mother's view there was still time for that. To her, the German language was more important, and all her life she saw to it that correct, formal German was spoken at home—she did not tolerate the colloquial Bukovinian dialect. So they agreed not to begin Paul's Jewish education until he had reached elementary school age.

In the autumn of 1926, a barely six-year-old Paul entered elementary school. He spent the first school year at the Meisler Institute, which included a four-year co-educational primary school with German instruction. There he was "well-behaved and quiet, but not a good student."[32] What was hidden within him was not yet revealed, and the paternal intimidations still inhibited the boy's willingness to learn.

Later, as a high school student, Paul would have liked to erase from his life the three school years that followed, just prior to his entrance in the Gymnasium.* For he had had to attend the Safah-Ivriah Hebrew school for three years against his will. His father wished it. He could also no longer afford the expensive tuition for the Meisler school. The Hebrew school was supported by Zionist organizations and was thus able to waive fees. In addition, this school corresponded to the father's educational principles.[33]

But Paul was unhappy. The Hebrew language of instruction and the noisy group of children repelled him. In the Meisler school everything had been quiet and decorous. He felt bound by constraints, which gradually increased his strength for revolt, although he would not succeed in rebelling until he was fourteen. In the Gymnasium he initially still had to learn Hebrew, although from a private tutor, the popular Mr. Rabinowicz. During that time he concealed his earlier attendance at the Hebrew school from his friends. As a Left-leaning student he must have found the memory of his "Zionist past" particularly disturbing.

For Paul's father, Hebrew was a second mother tongue. He had learned it early on at the religion school, the Cheder. For Paul, it was to become a "father tongue," which he would later reject along with everything else that came from his father. In addition to Hebrew, Paul also had to learn Romanian, which

---

*A *Gymnasium* usually comprises the last two years of elementary school (the fifth and sixth grades) plus junior high and high school (U.S.). —M.B.

had by then become the obligatory state language. That young Paul had to devote himself to the learning of two foreign languages was not a problem as far as his father was concerned.

Paul, the overtaxed elementary school student, found comfort in the short walk home from school, located in the nearby Färbergasse. It led through streets lined with chestnut trees, past gardens and flowers. Paul attentively watched the straying dogs and fleeing cats that crossed his path.

What he could not get from the Hebrew school, he found at home with his cousins. From them he learned Schiller's *Die Bürgschaft* and *Das Lied von der Glocke* by heart, even before he was able to read these poems himself. He had already begun to learn to read German at the Meisler school, and he continued to practice at home with the fairy tale books he received for his birthday from Aunt Berta in Vienna.

Paul did not seem to have any friends at elementary school. Cramped living conditions at the Antschels' and the strict household duties that Paul had to obey did not leave much room for friendships. Paul was not permitted to invite schoolmates home, and since he was under constant adult supervision, visits on his own initiative became impossible. On some Sundays and holidays, he and his parents visited Grandfather Schrager and Paul's young uncles Esriel and Bruno. They loved their little nephew and found amusing activities for him while the adults chatted.

At Grandfather Schrager's, Saturday evenings were celebrated according to tradition. Together with the old man the children sang the Havdala, a song about the separation of the holy Sabbath from mundane weekdays. The traditional melody gave Paul the rare opportunity to put his finely-tuned ear and beautiful voice to good use. On some Saturday evenings they would all visit the grandfather's brother, whose granddaughter, little Selma Meerbaum, would join the choir.[34]

Later in the girls' high school, the fifteen-year-old Selma, born in Czernowitz in 1924, began to write lyrical nature and love poems in German. At barely eighteen she died of typhus in Michailovka on the Bug River, in the same labor camp in which Paul's parents were held.[35] The following three, short stanzas are from "Poem," her most extensive composition:

. . .

I want to live.
I want to laugh and carry burdens
and want to fight and love and hate
and want to take hold of the sky with my hands
and want to be free and breathe and scream.

I don't want to die. No!
No.
Life is red,
Life is mine.
Mine and thine.
Mine.

Why do the cannons roar?
Why does life die for glittering coins?
. . .[36]

In Czernowitz Selma's grandmother accompanied the young singers on the piano. The musical evenings spent at the Schragers' revived Paul's mother's memory of a childhood dream which never became reality. Now, at least Paul's musical talents were to be cultivated and, as a piano was unaffordable, a cheaper instrument was to be procured. Thus they bought a child's violin and engaged a music teacher from the neighborhood. The music stand stood for several months in the small open space in the livingroom-bedroom, but Paul did not enjoy reading music, and despite his good ear he made no progress on the violin. Even playing the violin was a constraint to Paul! To his mother's disappointment, the music lessons had to be abandoned.[37]

Two months before his tenth birthday, in the fall of 1930, Paul entered the Gymnasium; he had easily passed the required entrance exam. The Liceul Ortodox de Băeți was a Romanian state school which had been known, even under Austrian rule, as the Eastern Orthodox Oberrealgymnasium. A stronghold of Romanian nationalism, it enjoyed the reputation of providing a solid education and had always been the school of choice for the Romanian elite. In the early thirties, as in the Austrian era, Jews were admitted but not very welcome. Still, many Jewish families sent their children to this best state school, since full command of the Romanian national language was a prerequisite for professional success. Instruction in the Jewish religion was obligatory at all schools, so his parents had little to worry about in this respect. In addition, Paul continued to learn Hebrew with his tutor. In a letter to his aunt in Vienna, Paul bitterly complained that he had to keep up his studies of this language even during Christmas vacation.[38]

Initially, everything went well at the Gymnasium. The teachers became aware of Paul's talents, his diligence and his eagerness, and appreciated him. Paul even had the ambition to become head of the class. Since there were more than a few talented students in his class, Paul had to fight for this position. This was easiest for Paul in the language classes. The Romanian teacher praised Paul's vocabulary and correct pronunciation, which was uncommon among Jewish students, and his French teacher was astonished at his linguistic talent. The professors always preferred to let Paul read poems aloud in class. His essays were often presented to the whole class as model compositions. The descriptive natural sciences were among Paul's favorite subjects, since in earlier years he had enjoyed observing plants, stones, and animals. Only in mathematics did Paul have to overcome difficulties in his third and fourth years at school; he was then tutored at home by his cousins. In the first two years, however, Paul managed to hold his own at the top of all his classes.

As such, Paul also had to take on the function of "monitor" or supervisor, and he took his post very seriously. He proudly carried the exercise books into the classroom, saw to strict silence in the class before the professor's arrival, and did not hesitate to report every student's misdeed, whether committed in class or during the break. If someone was punished as a consequence, then all of Paul's classmates turned against him. So for a long time many of his schoolmates avoided him or even hated him, considering him ambitious and a teacher's pet. Paul, however, was convinced of the correctness of his actions.[39]

Paul spent the summer vacation of 1931 with his relatives in Milie, in the parental home of Klara and Emma Nagel. But his stay in the countryside gave him more than his relatives' loving attention—during this vacation he found a friend. His name too was Paul, and he came from Vienna.

Paul Schafler and Paul Antschel were cousins once removed. His Viennese cousin came nearly every year with his parents to visit his maternal grandparents, David and Berta Katz. They were landowners in the village of Milie, but also had a house with a backyard in the city, located in the Metzgergasse. The Wassilkogasse, where the Antschels lived, led into this street. The Antschel and Schafler families met either at "Aunt Katz's," as they used to say in the family, or in the Antschel apartment. So, in the city, the young Pauls had often gotten together to play. A real friendship, however, did not develop until later, in the village. The Viennese visitors tended to spend part of their summers there, on the Katz family's estate, and when Paul Antschel stayed in the following years in Milie, he was a guest of the Katzes or Nagels.

That the Viennese cousin was younger than Paul and called "little Paul" as opposed to "big Paul," did not bother him at all. Paul Schafler writes, in recollection of their childhood together:

> I loved and adored Paul because of his behavior toward me. He was . . ., through his natural abilities and because of his certainly more difficult childhood, more mature and experienced. But there was never even a trace of condescension, which is actually normal in children of this age and age difference. He was always gentle and friendly, even loving to me and always treated me as an equal. . . . Our childhood friendship is still very much present in my mind. It was and is an important and wonderful part of my life.

And about the time spent in the countryside, Schafler says:

> We rode on horseback together, played soccer, prowled through the greens, paths, and fields of this region, which I . . . still consider to be my home.[40]

"We rode on horseback"—for Paul Antschel, riding, even

on the backs of the gentle Carpathian Hutsuls must have been an experience of freedom.[41] And when was Paul as close to nature, which he had already loved to observe as a child, as during the incomparable days at Milie? "Little Paul" was not only his playmate, to whom he owed his experiences at the estate, but was at the same time the younger brother Paul Antschel had so ardently wished for.

So it is hardly surprising that the mere family relationship did not suffice—especially not for Paul. "As children we initiated a blood brotherhood, consciously thinking of Karl May, * after which he was my brother Old Shatterhand and I was his brother Winnetou," Paul Schafler recounts.[42] What they had read remained conscious. What went on in Paul Antschel's unconscious can only be imagined.

Among the presents Paul's Viennese relatives had brought him was a traditional Tyrolean-style jacket, which fit him well. Paul, who was always concerned with his appearance and would not tolerate a spot or stain on his clothes, was delighted with this present. In later years he received the same kind of suit from Vienna. The Tyrolean jacket with green lapels—a rarity in the Bukovina—became Paul's trademark until his last years in the Gymnasium. His circle of female friends, which was to form a few years later, found the unusual clothing particularly appealing. The traditional suit was also a link with Vienna, the city of Paul's longing.[43]

The holidays in Milie over the next years lost nothing; rather, the experience gained in intensity. The last visit of the

---

*Karl May (1842–1912), best-selling German author who popularized stories of the Wild West and Red Indians. His main characters, white adventurer Old Shatterhand and his Sioux friend, Winnetou, were widely-known (and still are) by the youth of Central and Western Europe; a possible equivalent influence in the English-speaking world would be James Fenimore Cooper and his stories of the frontiersman Natty Bumppo. —M.B.

relatives from Vienna was in 1937—a few months before the German Reich's annexation of Austria and the Schaflers' escape to England. The cousins would not see each other again until after the Second World War—but their relations did not change. On this Paul Schafler writes: "In the year 1950, when I visited him in Paris, I—who had been raised in England since 1938, had served in the war as a soldier with the RAF and was accustomed to British restraint—greeted him holding out my hand; but he embraced and kissed me. I can still see his face before me, glowing with joy."[44]

For his twelfth birthday Paul received—probably from his uncle Bruno, the one who recited poems—a book which, despite its strangeness, would be of lasting influence. It was the book of Jewish "fables" by Eliezer Steinbarg, richly decorated with wood engravings by Arthur Kolnik and bound in cloth. Paul never spoke Yiddish, but like all Bukovinians he had an ear for the language, and the Hebrew alphabet, in which Yiddish texts are printed, was well-known to him. He began to read it immediately. The fable he liked most was that of the spear and the needle. The dispute over the differences between their jobs ends with the needle's words: "If I prick cloth, a shirt or a dress comes of it; if you prick people, what could possibly become of them?!"[45]

Paul learned the fable by heart and recited it enthusiastically to his family and friends; he was much admired and praised. After years of suppression, Steinbarg's fables were to resurface in Paul's mind precisely when the very existence of Judaism was most endangered.

Two events from Paul's childhood that seem worth mentioning have been retold without specific dates. Paul was once playing with some girls younger than he in the garden belonging to his "uncle Gottlieb." During the game of "tag," Paul caught the prettiest girl and wanted to hold her tightly to him. She, however, warded him off brusquely and ran to Uncle Gottlieb to tell on Paul. This was not the first time that the girls felt they had to be careful of Paul. Once earlier he had wanted to lure them into the cellar of his own house. He promised to show them something very "mysterious." But the little girls had refused to follow him. This time the girls' complaint had serious consequences for Paul: he was told to leave the garden and was never again permitted to set foot in it.[46]

Paul's cousin Edith told of more unusual occurrences. At times she would play with him in the apartment when his parents were not home. Sometimes Paul would suddenly cry out: "I'm afraid, Death is coming for me! I have to hide from him!" He would quickly crawl into his crib, which stood in his parents' bedroom and which he used until he was twelve years old. He would then hide under the blanket. Edith remembers having been terribly afraid herself.[47]

IV

Growth

Wachstum.	Growth.
Herzwand um Herzwand	Heartwall upon heartwall
blättert hinzu.	adds petals to it.

P AUL'S thirteenth year, 1933, brought an improvement in the Antschel family's standard of living. Cousins Klara and Emma Nagel had reached high-school age and had left the house and the city. Aunt Minna married and moved with her husband to Palestine. The apartment in the Wassilkogasse was now entirely at the disposal of Paul's parents. Paul obtained a room of his own, overlooking the street with its chestnut trees, and a sofa bed—the crib disappeared.

The fourth year in the lower level of the Gymnasium, which Paul had begun in the fall of 1933, marked an important division in the Romanian school system. Along with the final exam of the lower level, the "Little Baccalaureate," the student's aptitude to move into the upper level was evaluated in this year. Paul had to work hard to maintain merely a mediocre grade in mathematics.[48] He experienced no difficulties in the other subjects, although these also required some diligence. In order to find one's way, for example, among the dizzying numbers of Moldavian-Wallachian hospodars, or ruling princes, who were installed and removed by the Turks like marionettes in a puppet theater, great perseverance was needed. Paul had enough self-discipline to hold out. His own room, in which he was able to work undisturbed, was surely an important factor. What helped him the most, however, was his exemption from additional Hebrew lessons, which he managed to wring out of his father in the course of this year. This meant more than extra time for his studies; it was his first act of open rebellion against his father. His mother's support at the time probably played a significant part.

But before he succeeded, Paul had to make one more concession—the last one that he would grant his father. At the age of thirteen, he had to participate in a religious ceremony, which carries the same name as the participant—Bar Mitzvah (son of the commandment)—and is organized according to the ancient traditions of Judaism.[49] First, the Bar Mitzvah teacher came to the house for one week, an old Orthodox Jew with a long beard and side-locks. He taught Paul the prayers that are to be spoken in the synagogue before the unrolling and during the rolling up of the Torah, and rehearsed with him the chanting that is part of the reading from the Holy Scriptures. On the morning of his thirteenth birthday, the young Jewish boy participates in the service for the first time as a full member of the praying community of at least ten men—the Minyan—and he is called before the others to read from the Torah, the five books of Moses written in Hebrew on calfskin. Now considered fully of age, the Jew henceforth has to bind on his brow and his left arm the "tefillin," or phylacteries, before his weekday morning prayers. These phylacteries consist of leather thongs and small black leather boxes, which hold the creed written on parchment. One such box is bound around the brow with the attached black thong, the other placed on the left arm and its thong wrapped around and along the arm in a very specific manner. This ceremonial act is accompanied by the stipulated prayers. The entire procedure has to be learned perfectly and practiced intensively, since no mistakes may be made. The practical part of the instruction is supplemented by theoretical lessons on the commandments and restrictions of Judaism, since the Jew, from his Bar Mitzvah day on, is on his own and solely responsible for the fulfillment of the divine commandments. Because the boy's father is to some extent relieved of responsibility for his son's actions on this day, he says in the synagogue after the ceremony: "Lord, mayst Thou be praised, for Thou hast now freed me from him!"

Above all, it was Paul who felt truly freed after this day. He found no interest and certainly no joy in the whole ceremony and was only motivated by the fear of disgracing himself in the synagogue. He never again donned the phylacteries nor did he ever actively participate in another service.

On the day of this celebration, a surprise awaited Paul at home—a birthday present that gave him great joy. Friends of his parents, the Bittmanns, brought him Goethe's *Faust* in a beautiful two-volume edition partly bound in leather. Paul sat down to read immediately, and as long as his parents' home existed, the two volumes lay on his desk. After many years, Paul was to have the chance to thank these friends a second time for their thoughtful gift. In 1947, having just fled Romania completely without resources, he was forced to ask to be taken in by these acquaintances who were then living in Vienna. [50]

In the poetry of Celan's maturity, one finds reminiscences

of his Bar Mitzvah when he writes: "... we, / ten in number, sand people...." The poet supplements this, in a way, in the closing lines of another poem:

Schwarz, phylakterien- farben, so wart ihr, ihr mit- betenden Schoten.	Black, phylactery- colored, so were you, you pods joining the prayers.

On a third occasion, the picture is completed:

... hinsingend über auf-, auf-, auf- geblättertes Bibelgebirg, ...	... singing their way over Bible ranges flicked open, open, open, ...[51]

At the end of 1933 Paul first heard a live report of the persecution of the Jews in the German Reich after Hitler's rise to power. His uncle David, his father's brother, had to leave Germany and wanted to start anew in his native Romanian home. He was a guest at his brother's for a few weeks before settling in Bucharest. Paul listened attentively to the stories his uncle told and began to have an idea of the Nazis' persecution of the Jews. At the same time he was amazed at his uncle's pronunciation of German as it was spoken in the Reich, which sounded strangely foreign to him. David, a jovial man, enjoyed listening to Paul's reports on the conditions in Romanian schools, and the two became "the best of friends," as Paul wrote in a letter to his aunt in Palestine. This letter, the only one

Growth

that has survived from Paul's childhood, says the following:

Czernowitz, January 30th 1934

Dear aunt Minna!
Most of all, please forgive my not writing. I don't have any motivation for that either. So, *pardonnez-moi*, please!
Concerning the matter of grade sheets, yes, hm, I'm the second, but. . . . not the first, as it should have rightfully been. The professors, my belonging to the *Jewish* branch of the *Semitic* race, and many other obstacles! Yes, concerning anti-Semitism in our school, I could write a 300-page book about it. As an example, let me just offer you the fact that my geography professor, Zoppa is the devil's name, has been "inside" for two months, where, you can surely imagine.
You probably know that uncle David is already here. I get along very well with him. We're even the best of friends.
Unfortunately I could not go to school today since I fell yesterday on the ice and hurt my bottom pretty badly. Let it be said for your peace of mind, that it will be alright soon. It is thanks to this first circumstance that you are already now getting a reply; otherwise, who knows when. . . . .
Aunt Regina has been coming to see us often recently.
How are you? Have you found some work? How is it with the apartment? Please write about it.
And how is it going with the languages? *Speake-you*

Paul Celan

English? And Hebrew?
 With kind regards and kisses
 I remain Your
 Paul

P. S. Regards to Donia.
 D. U.

In the margin is written: "You're in Palestine now! Please send me stamps from there and other foreign ones. You know that I'm a stamp-collector."[52]

Professor Zoppa, who was in jail at the time, was the leader of the Czernowitz "Garda de Fier" (Iron Guard). Initially the group, which had been directly influenced by National Socialism, merely instigated riots against Jewish students at the University. Later, however, it plotted against the Romanian government which was still allied with the Western powers. Zoppa was arrested because of this political conspiracy. But according to reports from former schoolmates of Paul's, Zoppa is said to have behaved correctly in school. He recognized that Paul was one of the best, if not *the* best, of his geography students. It was not Zoppa, but rather mathematics that were the reason Paul did not remain at the top of his class.

Zoppa is said to have once used his good knowledge of Yiddish to mock the students' "jargon." Paul protested: "A valuable body of literature exists in the Yiddish language, and great works of world literature, yes, even Shakespeare has been translated into this language!" Contemptuously, Zoppa replied: "How funny these translations must be! Even the simple Yiddish sentence 'Kim aher' ['Come here'] sounds ridiculous!" Paul did not admit defeat and answered: "The Romanian translation of this sentence is also simply ridiculous. What does 'Vino'n coa' sound like, after all?" The teacher gave Paul the last word and was silent. Paul must certainly have permitted himself this exchange—no onc clsc in the class would have dared—only because he considered his position with Zoppa secure.[53]

The history professor Zub, who was otherwise unprejudiced, allowed himself an even more biting comment on the Jews. During a lecture on Romanian national endeavors, Zub remarked in an aside that Jews could in fact never understand the meaning of patriotism because they had no home. A quickwitted Paul interjected: "But we gave humanity the book of all books." Again, a teacher had to accept his student's objection silently. And Paul, the best-versed history student, was conscious of his strength and superiority.[54]

In June of 1934 Paul passed the graduating exam of the lower Gymnasium without difficulty and was given his parents' permission to spend his holidays in the mountains. He went with a boy of his age whom he had known little until then. Manuel was the son of family friends, the Singers. Together, the parents had planned their sons' venture. The Antschels, who could not afford a vacation of their own, trusted Manuel Singer, a sensible and very practical boy, with the responsibility for Paul. Together they spent two weeks hiking, swimming and talking in a village in southern Bukovina. Thus began Paul's friendship with Manuel, his future fellow student in Tours.[55]

The transformations Paul underwent in the years 1933 and 1934 affected his relationships with his fellow students. He was no longer the best student nor the class monitor, but just a boy like all the others who sought companionship and tried to encourage friendship. Paul was attractive and had an engaging way of speaking. He also proved to be a helpful schoolmate, who, even during class, allowed others to copy from his notebook.

The first classmate with whom Paul joined up was Gustav Chomed, known as Gustl. Gustl had observed him from a distance for a long time because of his "intelligence and good looks." Due to his shyness, Gustl had not dared to address Paul until the desired circumstance arose as if by chance. One morning, the natural sciences teacher did not show up for class, and the students sat idly in the classroom, chatting quietly. As the class's seating order was not respected in this room, Paul and Gustl happened to sit together. Gustl finally worked up the courage to speak to Paul, and the two became friends. Since Paul now had his own room, he was able to invite friends home. Gustl stood up firmly to Paul's mother's scrutinizing look and became a welcome guest. [56] But not every young boy was as willing to let himself be observed so critically by a friend's parent. Ernst Engler, another schoolmate, recounts that he felt very oppressed in the presence of Paul's mother. She struck him as a strict governess who observed her pupil with Argus eyes. [57]

Paul was surely more comfortable in Gustl's parental home because there they had more freedom. In the large courtyard there was an old water-well where they could pass the time drawing water. It was fun to turn the heavy wooden wheel, to lift the wooden pail over the well's rim, bring it out of the well-house and pour water into the prepared buckets. All this still existed only at the Chomeds' in the Töpfergasse, which lay in an outer district of the city. Down the nearby Feldgasse, one could stroll all the way to the train tracks and the green fields at the city limits. And in winter, the Töpfergasse with its steep incline was ideal for sledding.

Growth

Erich Einhorn joined Paul and Gustl, becoming the third member of the group. Erich, who was not a schoolmate of theirs but attended a private Gymnasium, was related to Paul as members of their families had married. For Paul's interest in Erich the mere difference in their appearances was probably decisive: Erich had blond hair, blue eyes, and broad shoulders. Paul, dark-haired, with brown eyes, and a delicate build, offered a striking contrast to Erich, which was underscored by their very different characters. Erich was always in a good mood, and, contrary to Paul's, his smile was always wide and friendly. Paul, who only rarely smiled and then usually out of embarrassment, was very much subject to wide changes of mood. Although both could be considered comfortable and spoiled, there was one large difference: Erich, the son of rich parents, had surely experienced a more carefree and less problematic childhood than Paul.

The families' social differences played no role in the relationship of the three friends. Gustl's father was a master tailor, Erich's a lawyer, and Paul's father was most likely the economically weakest among them. Erich lived on the Springbrunnenplatz in his old family home, with private rooms and lawyer's chambers on the extensive second floor. The Chomeds lived in their own small house in the rural Töpfergasse. The Antschels' gloomy ground-floor apartment in the Wassilkogasse was without a doubt the poorest. But these differences did not bother the adolescents at all.[58]

In early September 1934 Uncle David, who was then living in Bucharest, came to Czernowitz to spend the Jewish holidays, the New Year celebrations, and Yom Kippur with them. He was a confirmed bachelor and his family sentiments were aroused only during holidays. When he returned home to Bucharest, he took his nephew Paul for several days, with whom he continued to get along well. Paul had not yet seen the Romanian capital and so was delighted to accompany his uncle. Impressions from this first trip to Bucharest are possibly found in an early undated poem Paul initially named "Whence," but later entitled "In the Park."[59]

Paul had gradually grown out of the confinement of his youth and now proved more independent, open-minded, and sociable.

V

There Was a Freedom

Es war,
und bisweilen wusstest auch du's,
es war
eine Freiheit.

There was,
And at times you knew it too,
there was
a freedom.

AT the beginning of the 1934–1935 school year—his fifth year in the Gymnasium and his first in the upper level—Paul changed to another school.[60] He left the Liceul Ortodox de Băeți, not because of the curriculum, which was standardized in Romanian high schools, but simply because of the rampant anti-Semitism. His parents probably thought that Paul's great sensitivity was behind his severe judgment of his professors. They nonetheless allowed themselves to be influenced by the general effort of Jewish students to leave schools with anti-Semitic tendencies, and supported Paul's decision. An additional and decisive circumstance was that Manuel Singer, who until then had attended the Third State Gymnasium, also wanted to change schools. This former Jewish Gymnasium, which was still almost exclusively attended by Jewish students, was neglected by the Romanian authorities and had correspondingly low teaching standards. As a result, Manuel proposed that Paul and he attend the Liceul Marele Voevod Mihai, a state Gymnasium, named after the royal successor to the king, Crown Prince Michael.

This former Ukrainian Gymnasium had the reputation of being the city's most liberal school, but also of having "hardworking teachers of the old style,"[61] who passed a sound body of knowledge on to their students. The teachers were for the most part Ukrainians, who had received a German-language education and whose first educational experiences were acquired during the Habsburg Monarchy. A few Jews also remained on the faculty from the Austrian days, and the administration was able to choose new Romanian professors from democratically-inclined circles that were unsympathetic to anti-Semitism. In Romania of the 1930s and especially in the Bukovina, these were nearly ideal conditions.

In addition, the majority of the students at the Ukrainian state Gymnasium were Jews, since the Ukrainians of the Bukovina preferred to send their children to emphatically nationalistic Romanian schools. Unlike other nationalities, they were easily assimilated into the Romanian nation, due to their common Eastern Orthodox or Catholic-Orthodox religions and the similarity of their family names. Also, most of them had abandoned the idea of a pan-Slavic confederation after 1922, when a large part of the Ukraine had fallen to the "Bolshevik" Soviet Union. Thus, few were interested in the Ukrainian language instruction available at the state Gymnasium.

Among the twenty-eight students in Paul's class, only nine were Ukrainian. The rest were Jewish and this greatly affected the tenor of the class. Nonetheless, the entire four years up to the graduation exam were marked by great harmony between

Jews and non-Jews. The professors also proved tolerant, although this did not diminish their strict educational stance.

The director, Tudan, also taught Latin to Paul's class. He was a typical representative of the old Austrian humanists: thorough and pedantic in his lectures and examinations, he wanted to teach his students roughly the same knowledge of Latin grammar and syntax that he had acquired. Those who had attended his lectures testify without exception to Tudan's correctness and fairness. In addition, he was one of the last members of the generation of Ukrainians and Jews who collaborated harmoniously in the German-language cultural life of the Bukovina.

History and geography were taught by a Romanian, named Migula, whose open-mindedness allowed him to discuss questions of differing conceptions of history and other methods of historiography with Paul. Paul's views often differed considerably from those expressed in the text books.

The Romanist and poet Aurel Vasiliu taught Romanian. Although he published his poems under a pseudonym in Romanian journals, he was soon identified by his students. Vasiliu did not know that the student Antschel wrote poems in German, but recognized his strong interest in languages in general and particularly in Romanian, in which Paul read a great deal in the upper level. Since the teacher noticed that Paul did not study languages and literature merely as required subjects, the two would occasionally tackle literary themes which remained incomprehensible to the other students.[62]

Two professors were then to become Paul's "victims": the French teacher, who spoke the language of Corneille and Racine with a light Ukrainian accent, had to let Paul correct him; and the German professor, a Jewish Germanist of the old school, could not defend himself against Paul's expositions of

Paul Celan

German literary themes except by exclaiming: "Drop it, would you, you are too bright for me!"[63]

The beginning of his German instruction, which did not start until the sixth Gymnasium grade, or the second year in the upper level, was associated with an unusual incident. The Romanian curriculum called for beginning German instruction, and the text books were written accordingly. But since all the Jewish students had German as a mother tongue and the language was foreign only to the small number of Ukrainians, the professor's naive attempt to follow the prescribed program was met with amusement and mockery on the part of the Jews. Finally however, it came to a revolt, which prompted the despairing teacher to seek help from the school director. The latter was understanding towards the students' request and obtained an extraordinary edict from the Ministry of Education, which made it possible for students who spoke German to enjoy German instruction according to the old Austrian curriculum. Thus, during the three years before the graduation exam, the history of German literature was taught from its beginnings to the Romantics, and the students read classics such as Lessing, Goethe, Schiller, and Kleist.

Paul's new hobby was sketching, which was taught once a week. One of his former schoolmates, who used to visit him at home, remembers Paul's efforts to draw burning candles. The candle's successive phases of burning and being extinguished preoccupied Paul intensely.[64] During this time, Paul was also enraptured by Rodin's sculptures.

Despite his delicate appearance, Paul was healthy and strong. He was accomplished in gymnastics on the parallel bars, the horizontal bar, and the vaulting horse. He liked to play handball, was a good swimmer, and ice-skated in the winter. Occasionally he also played tennis.

There Was a Freedom

In his last two years of school, Paul's class was divided into a "literary" section—actually humanistic—and a natural science section. Paul naturally chose the literary-humanistic one, in which Greek was added to existing Latin instruction, but mathematics and physics were dropped. He was finally free of the subjects he disliked. The two groups continued to share instruction in Romanian, history, geography, French, preparatory philosophy, and, in the last year, sociology. Religious instruction for the Jews, which was conducted in Romanian—Hebrew was not at all in the curriculum—included biblical and Jewish history. The Jewish religion teacher, however, was originally a Germanist.

In the last years, Paul gave priority to his extensive personal reading over his' homework. He gradually came to view his presence at school as a necessary evil, a prerequisite for university studies, and lost the ambition to work for high grades. When these did not come automatically, as they did in German, French, history or geography, he was content with a "Sufficient," which allowed him to move on to the next class. In this way he advanced undisturbed.

At home and in tedious classes, he read German, French, and Romanian literature, world history, and the descriptive natural sciences, especially botany. He spent more and more of his free afternoons in the libraries of the Toynbee Hall and the university, rummaging in massive volumes, encyclopedias, dictionaries and specialized studies in a variety of fields. Better-read than any of his schoolmates, he was always ahead of them. If Corneille and Racine were being studied, he was already reading Verlaine and Rimbaud; and if the class was still working on Schiller and Goethe, he had already reached Hölderlin and Rilke. Paul was increasingly respected by his fellow students—some admired him as a walking encyclopedia, others saw in him a stimulating example. Although the teachers occasionally entered into discussions with Paul, and despite his brilliance, they never could forgive him one thing: his indifference toward the material currently being covered. The class as a whole, however, felt elated and honored when Paul shone in its presence; yet there were a few envious students who tried, even if in vain, to match him.

In 1935 the Antschel family home underwent another transformation. They moved into a house they had bought in a new neighborhood, in the Masarykgasse. The family chose this part of town because Paul's Gymnasium was in the immediate vicinity. On the way into the city center Paul could walk along the Splenygasse, another avenue lined with chestnut trees, considered the most beautiful in the city.[65]

Everyone was satisfied with the move. Paul's father had finally been able to fulfill his wife's long-standing wish for a comfortable, modern house. His mother was happy with the bright, newly-furnished home, and Paul was able to look forward to more frequent visits from his friends, who, in fact, came more readily. Like the family, they also felt more at ease one floor above number 10 Masarykgasse than in the old, gloomy apartment.

The exterior changes, however, could not hide the change in the family's internal relations. Leo Antschel and his wife continued to live in apparently perfect harmony, but in truth they were more and more alienated. Fritzi Antschel became completely wrapped up in her love for her son. When friends came to visit him, she stayed with them, participated in their conversations or listened, enraptured, to Paul. She made sure her guests were as comfortable as possible and made an effort to appear as young in behavior as her son and his guests.

It was also clear to all of Paul's friends that he worshipped his mother. During puberty, Paul's early, childish love for his mother had developed into an intensive fixation, which now dominated his entire emotional life. Everything coarsely sexual was either repressed or converted into an ideal romantic attachment to his mother. In this way, his mother's affection for him corresponded to Paul's love for her.

Paul completely detached himself emotionally from his father and began to view him only as an extra in the house. He rejected the old man's "petit-bourgeois" Zionism,[66] and even despised his subservient and, in Paul's eyes, "dirty" work as a broker. He did not hesitate to voice his opinion to his friends.[67] However, the true roots of these feelings are probably to be found in the strict education of his early youth, in the severe punishments and the many constraints. That Leo Antschel, a simple, honest, but professionally plagued man, could not become a role model in Paul's life seems understandable in light of Paul's varied talents. Yet the causes must have run much deeper for Paul to have wanted to exclude his father so completely from his own life.[68]

Initially, "stormy arguments" are said to have taken place between father and son,[69] although not because of Paul's indifference toward religion and Hebrew—his father eventually came to terms with that—but because of the new liberties Paul had begun to take, at least since 1935. One of them was that Paul often stayed out late at night without his father's permission. But even worse, he had acquired during this time a leftist view of the world, which was constantly the topic of discussions among his friends and also was not kept hidden from his father. For Leo Antschel there was probably no thought more horrible than that Paul might one day land in jail for political activities. His father had no idea how wide the gap between belief and action was in Paul's case! Finally though, he had to admit he was powerless to change Paul's views and behavior, and he gave up the struggle. He avoided further discussions, and when Paul's friends were present, he retreated into his room.

The first stimulus for Paul's social and political reflections probably came from his uncle Esriel, who at university had given up his studies of the Talmud in favor of his interest in Marx and Engels. Esriel frequented socialist circles and, whenever Paul visited, he found him arguing with his friends. It surely took some time for Paul, to move from listening to asking questions, but it seems that the introduction to Marxism Paul received through his uncle must have been unsatisfactory. In the summer of 1935, he encountered a former schoolmate, who had gone from the Zionist Youth group over to the Communists and was considered "revolutionary" by his friends. Paul immediately asked him why there were different socialist parties, who all referred to Marx, and what differentiated them from one another. This time Paul must have received what seemed to him a satisfactory reply, since he attended an illegal meeting of the Anti-Fascist Youth that summer.[70]

The meeting took place outside in the Cecina forest and was organized by circles dedicated to the anti-fascist education of the young. The main presentation was given by a Czernowitz student from Bucharest University, who had been brought specifically because the meeting was to be conducted in German. The participants were almost exclusively Jewish high school boys and girls between the ages of fifteen and eighteen. The speaker outlined the political situation in the world and in Romania, and discussed the threat to democratic nations from growing militant fascism, promoted by Germany. He closed with the confident explanation that only the Soviet Union was capable of guaranteeing the victory of the proletariat over fascism. During the discussion, Paul raised his hand. His scepticism concerning the Soviet Union was not new to the speaker—these doubts were often expressed similarly—but Paul's splendid formulation and the beauty of his speech impressed him very much, and he decided to keep an eye on the strange boy. Indeed, a few years later the two were to meet again and become friends.[71]

Paul now regularly took part in an anti-fascist circle that met in private homes. The parents of these youths either did not know why the children met, or they had nothing against their political activities. Paul participated little in the debates; usually he sat silently in a corner and listened attentively. Nevertheless, members of the group were proud of his presence. He must have had such a powerful aura that there was even talk of his "charisma."[72]

What Paul heard, however, was unsatisfactory. He began to read Marx's *Das Kapital* and the "Communist Manifesto," but did not derive much pleasure from them. Nor did Engels' writings satisfy him. He gained little from "the fathers of Socialism" and was especially repelled by their arid materialism. A different book, which he came upon by chance, appealed to him immediately: the anarchist prince Peter Kropotkin's *Mutual Charity*. In this book he found the warm humanity and appreciation of life that was so lacking in Marxism. He also read Kropotkin's *The Speeches of a Rebel*. Russian anarchism, which rebelled against the paternalistic Tsar, corresponded to Paul's own revolt against his father. His later declaration of sympathy with the exiled Trotsky, the outcast "son of the Revolution," leads one to assume an identification with the victim, the mistreated son of "Father Stalin."

The summer of 1935 was long and warm, and there was enough time for a holiday in Milie. This year, the Viennese relatives had canceled their visit there, so Paul invited his school friend Manuel Singer and they spent the rest of the vacation with the Nagel family.

The 1935–1936 school year was one of the happiest of Paul's youth: he had won many friends and the admiration of his fellow students, and he was respected by his teachers, even if he was no longer at the top of his class. They all surrounded him with affection, in which he felt as secure as in the love of his mother. Paul had found his own world and felt completely anchored in it, no matter how much his father "ranted and raved" at times, in the words of a close friend of Paul's.[73] A group photograph of the sixth Gymnasium class, taken before the end of the school year in the spring of 1936, shows a cheerful, smiling Paul, who clearly feels at ease. Gone is the sad seriousness on young Paul's face in the family picture of 1923!

At the outbreak of the Spanish civil war, Paul let himself be talked into political action for the first and last time. He collected donations for the "Red Help," which was to benefit the Republican fighters in Spain. Immediate human solidarity, however, meant much more to him than such political activities.

Paul spent the summer vacation of 1936 at his friend Erich Einhorn's uncle's sawmill in the mountain village of Frumosul. Since three of their common friends were vacationing at the same time in the neighboring village of Russ-Moldavitza, Paul insisted on hiking to the village, which was only accessible on foot, until Erich finally agreed. Paul longed for a larger circle of people, was engrossed at the time in Rilke's "Cornet," and wanted to share his thoughts. Thus they set out one evening, hiked through most of the night, and woke their friends in the morning. They greeted each other heartily, and during breakfast Paul read to them from the thin book. His friends heard this poem for the first time and seemed to share

There Was a Freedom

Paul's enthusiasm—at least they gave him the impression of being won over as disciples of Paul's new master.

But Paul was deeply disappointed when he tried to read from Rilke's *Book of Images* on another occasion. His friends no longer seemed understanding. On the next school excursion, he even had to listen to a parody of Rilke, which hurt him deeply. At that time, the excursion's destination had nearly been reached and everyone was hungrily awaiting the picnic. When someone began to recite: "Who is hungry now, somewhere in the world . . .", the group broke into laughter—except for Paul, who decided never again to read Rilke to his friends.[74] He sought more understanding, and found it among the opposite sex.

If Paul's appeal was evident among his school friends at the Gymnasium, what an effect he must have had on girls. His first friendship with a girl was strangely ambivalent, however, as is apparent in this report written 40 years later by the first female friend of his youth, Ilse.

> Our youth was anything but idyllic. . . . [I]t [is] common . . . to see the past in a romanticized light. Paul . . . deserves better. I met Paul when I was fifteen and he barely sixteen. We both had a certain reputation among our friends, each for different reasons. It was summer, I was swimming in the Prut and suddenly noticed that someone was persistently swimming after me, to the most dangerous spots—we were both good swimmers. Finally, absolutely miserable, he says: Miss, you misjudge me, I don't really want that, I'm following you for completely different reasons, for your ideas, I want to speak with you about your ideas. . . . A moment earlier the world had still been wonderful . . ., as he approached me, an icy shadow

75

fell over everything and stayed. His presence burdened me, and this never changed. I didn't like him from the first moment. My aversion . . . was physical. Even though . . . he [was] an unusually attractive person, completely in the style of a young Romantic, like Byron or Shelley, with the soft eyes of a deer and skin the tone of a gold-dusted peach, with long, slender, elegantly-proportioned limbs. One of his more understanding admirers compared him to a young alder, not unrightly so. At times it seemed to me that a sultriness surrounded him, like that in a greenhouse of orchids. He had a very girlish manner of tilting his head to the side and letting his glance drift melancholically, which made me angry. . . . In his whole being there was something effeminately weak and self-pitying . . . I found myself the more masculine. . . . I think it was this . . . confusion of gender which . . . gave rise . . . to a deep antipathy. In later years I realized—maybe I suspected it back then—that this is one of the ingredients, the curse and property of the poet, the creator: to stand between the sexes or to be of both. I also remember that he once acted out Ophelia's madness scene and Juliet's balcony scene for me. Astonishing. And I had the feeling: Now everything is clear. But it was very frightening. . . . Paul's political interests were never far away. . . . His relationship with me didn't play a role there at all. It was my hardness, consistency, and the narrow-mindedness which I had cultivated, which attracted him. . . . Paul was not very good at foreseeing the consequences of his supposed interests, which prompted my contempt. But for many facts and situations he had a surprisingly lively and critical eye, something of Hölderlin's capacity for premonition. . . . In fact, in these years he had a sense only for the extraordinary, which he completely fulfilled.[75]

After this experience of the "early and miserable years" of an ambivalent relationship, they would both, later as students, try again to "overcome our common experience . . . to find the way toward a decent friendship. . . ."[76]

Paul's second female friendship, which he probably began in the following year, 1937, went differently, and yet similarly. Edith had blue eyes and blond hair like Ilse, but she wore her braids pinned up in a bun, while Ilse allowed hers to hang free. Paul met Edith Horowitz at Gustav Chomed's, whose neighbor and playmate she had been in childhood. Edith's true friendship with Gustav had actually begun with their encounter in the "circle," and Paul now again became the "third in the group." The fact that Edith was less interested in worldly problems and more so in literature must have prompted Paul to take occasional walks with her. In addition, her father's library contained many treasures of German poetry. Dr. Horowitz, who had been active in the Austrian era as a Germanist, later refused to adjust to the Romanian language. He preferred instead to earn his living in a bank and study German privately. In his library Paul was allowed to browse freely, and in doing so, he came upon two books which would become very significant to him: a book of Hugo von Hofmannsthal's prose which included the "Letter from Lord Chandos" and the short-story collection, *A Country Doctor*, by Kafka.[77] The "Chandos Letter," which was heavily discussed in the Horowitz house, influenced Celan's early poetry. And Kafka, once discovered, was to hold him in a spell all his life. In his later years, Celan made Kafka part of his daily reading.[78]

When Paul began, in 1935 or 1936, to recite Rilke's poetry to a "readers' circle," which, aside from him, was made up entirely of girls, he became the girls' idol. They met at the girls' parents' homes, and Paul's melodious voice transported them into the world of the poet. Of course, most of the girls came because of Paul rather than Rilke, but at least they had to make an effort to share Paul's experience of the poetry. Decades later, some of his former listeners could still recite stanzas from Rilke, although they had not reread them since. Ruth Tal, for example, was considered Paul's third "sweetheart," because she accompanied him to dance evenings at the Davidia fraternity in the winter of 1937–1938 and played tennis with him in the spring of 1938. She has long been a mother and housewife without time for literary interests, but she remembers the image of the blind beggar in Rilke's poem, "Pont du Carrousel."[79]

The following report from Ruth Kaswan, a friend of Paul's in the thirties, is also illuminating:

I got to know Paul when we were both thirteen, but I do not remember the occasion. There was an 'adult,' who was eighteen or older—whose name escapes me—and a group surrounding him that had begun to study Marxism. . . . It was in 1934–37, and the events that concerned us were the rise of Hitler in Germany, the growing anti-Semitism in Romania, and the civil war in Spain. . . . [Paul] was very handsome, almost girl-like, an intellectual, delicately-built boy, who had no interest in sports and games. . . . In school it was expressly prohibited to speak anything but Romanian. Among us, however, we spoke only German. . . . At the same time, we read French.[80] Paul Verlaine was our chosen hero. We learned poems by heart and competed enthusiastically in finding poetic treasures.[81] After some time, we returned to Rimbaud.

There Was a Freedom

Of Rimbaud we particularly loved *A Season in Hell*. We
also read Gide. I remember *Fruits of the Earth* in particular. The only German poet we read was Rilke. We also
read a few Romanian works, mainly because we needed
them for school. We read intensively and passionately.
We also wrote. I know that I wrote in German, French,
and Romanian. And Paul was without a doubt at the
center of this activity. I don't remember much about Paul's
ability to recite, and have not retained any general impression from the poems he wrote in those days. I remember
that our standard was Verlaine—the images and the musical nature of his language. Form was very important, and
we were much more concerned with style than with content. We sincerely endeavored—feeling our way carefully—to find enlightenment. We studied rhyme and
meter. And even though we hadn't the slightest idea about
free verse, we were able to differentiate between doggerel
and poetry. I think we knew that because Paul taught us.
Our political convictions were romantic-communist, but
not very deep. And Paul's influence on us was great,
although he applied no pressure and was not authoritarian.
He did not tell us what to think, he simply knew much
more.[82]

Members of the reader's circle report that, between 1935
and 1938, Paul dedicated himself first to one, then to another
of his listeners, accompanied her home, or hiked with her to
the romantic Habsburgshöhe. But none of them was close to
Paul in the sense that one could speak—as those surrounding
him did—of an amorous relationship.[83] "Girls fell for him,"
they said, "but Paul did not know what to do with them." "Yes,
he was afraid of girls!"[84] If they showed no interest in aesthetic

Paul Celan

conversations, Paul would leave them. It seems he loved only one person: his mother. "Oh Mother: oh you one and only," Rilke's Malte Laurids Brigge once says.[85]

Paul did not stop with Rilke, he also turned to Trakl and Hölderlin. In the readers' circle, however, which had only been concerned with lyrical poetry, another of Paul's inclinations came to light: he wanted to be an actor. He had begun to read Shakespeare in German translation, and since he liked to read aloud, he again needed an audience. At first he tried to assign parts in the readers' circle, for which he also brought male friends. However, since all the participants proved useless, Paul read all the parts, both male and female, himself. With a voice "somewhere between mezzo-soprano and alto,"[86] Paul brought the characters of Hamlet and Ophelia, Romeo and Juliet to life without directors or sets. He acted these parts with rich gestures and mimicry, to the delight of his audience, though he seemed "uncanny" to them.[87] With obvious satisfaction, Paul accepted his audience's applause.

The young Czernowitz actor Jehuda Eren-Ehrenkranz had a lasting influence on Paul's acting ability. Paul could watch him recite in German and Yiddish at the student hostel in 1937. Paul's interest in the theater was awakened early, probably as early as his visits to the Yiddish theater in Czernowitz, to which he was taken by his uncle Bruno when he was twelve. Later, as a student, Paul saw the performances of classic Romanian plays in the city theater. In the mid-thirties, he finally was able to see German-language guest performances from Vienna and Transylvania and to attend performances of the German touring company of Romania, whose members were Jewish actors driven out of theaters in the German Reich.

Paul knew the classical French dramas and Shakespeare—which, in Romanian translation, was part of the Czernowitz theater's repertoire—from his classes at school, where the French authors at least were read in the original. These Romanian versions, however, did not satisfy him—he still preferred German translations. Paul turned increasingly to the originals. He had no difficulties with the French poets—he is said to have won first prize in a school essay-writing contest on French literature at fourteen.[88] But so that he would no longer be dependent on translations of English literature, Paul began in the winter of 1937–1938, his last year in school, to learn the language of Shakespeare.

His father approved, but only for practical reasons. At this time the Goga-Cuza Cabinet, the first ultra-nationalist government, directly influenced by German National Socialism, held the reigns of power in Bucharest, and Paul's father was seriously considering emigration to Palestine. The police ban in the winter of 1937–1938 on the anti-fascist youth group was clearly another impetus for his plans. Its members were let off with a severe warning because of their young age, but the parents feared further measures by the authorities. Paul worried little about this issue, mainly because the readers' circle was much more important to him than any political group. Nonetheless, Paul's parents wanted to rid him once and for all of his compromising desire to be a leftist student. Since his mother also applied pressure on him, Paul finally agreed to apply for admission to the Jewish-national Davidia fraternity. This was actually a "pre-fraternity," in which the high school students were prepared for the actual student fraternity.[89]

For one semester, Paul participated in their evening gatherings and drinking sessions, and sat through the brash and imperious speeches uneasily. The only consolation he found in this group were the dance evenings in the Boris Room, to which he was able to invite a girlfriend. But when the political situation in Romania became calmer with the fall of the Goga-Cuza regime in the spring of 1938, Paul immediately left the Davidia. His "like-minded friends" from the disbanded anti-fascist circle had not learned of his Zionist escapade, and in school only two or three friends, themselves members of Davidia, knew of Paul's brief appearance in the student society.

In the winter of 1937–1938 at the latest, Paul began to recite his own poems and to give them to his female friends. Although none of his male friends had seen any of his poems before, they all knew that he wrote them. To them, this activity seemed to be only a way of passing time in uninteresting classes. But in this second-to-last year in high school, one classmate, Immanuel Weissglas, would have given much to be allowed to read one of Paul's poems. He wrote poems of his own and was a good pianist, who played for school celebrations and for his friends at home. Paul, however, also denied him the chance of reading his poetry.[90]

The remaining students of Paul's class would not have been at all interested in the creations of their poetic schoolmates, had it not been for Weissglas's idea of translating the Romanian lyrical poet Mihai Eminescu's "Luceafărul" ("The Morning Star") into German and reading it to the class. When Paul announced that he would have done it differently, Weissglas challenged him to give a sample of his own work. Paul remained silent, but his fellow students were convinced that a "poetic competition" between the two was imminent. In reality, Paul neither challenged Weissglas then nor later. At times, Paul attended Weissglas' concerts for his schoolmates at his parents' hospitable home in a quiet street on the outskirts of town, but Paul deliberately avoided discussing poetry with him.[91] It was easy to limit the two "rivals'" encounters to such occasional meetings, since Weissglas, who "wanted to live only in his poetry and his art," was held back and then no longer Paul's classmate in his last years at the Gymnasium.[92]

The exact point at which Paul Antschel began to write poetry remains uncertain. Former schoolmates report that they learned of his poetry in the sixth Gymnasium year, at the latest, and early female friends claim to have received poems from him when he was only fifteen.

Three collections of poems from Paul's youth have been preserved: a typescript assembled by Paul and two friends in the spring of 1944 (from here on referred to as "Typescript 1944"), a collection hand-written by Paul between the fall of 1944 and early 1945 (here entitled "Manuscript 1944/45"), a typescript assembled by Ruth Lackner in 1957 from the poems Celan had left behind in Bucharest (here "Typescript 1957").[93] In these collections only a few poems are dated. The poem "Klage" (Complaint) has a note, "1938;" the comment "Mother's Day 1938" has been added to an untitled poem, which begins with the line "Kein ankerloses Tasten stört die Hand" ("No anchorless groping disturbs the hand"); a second untitled poem which begins, "Die Mutter, lautlos heilend" ("the mother, silently healing") is followed by the note "Mother's Day 1939;" the date "1939" appears without comment under the poem "Heimkehr" (Homecoming); and finally, the date of the composition of "Während der Reise" (While Travelling) can be deduced from the comment following the text, "In Northern Germany," since young Celan was in northern Germany only once: on his trip to Tours in the year 1938.[94]

In a small notebook of Paul's, however, twenty poem titles have been recorded with their dates.[95] But all of the dates, which are from the year 1943, actually mark the days, according to Ruth Lackner, on which Paul reconstructed from memory for her poems written earlier. This was during his time at the

Paul Celan

labor camp, when, in all of his letters to Ruth, Paul enclosed poems which he had written since his arrival there in July 1942.

The poems in "Typescript 1944" and in "Manuscript 1944/ 45" seem to be ordered, judging by style and content, more or less following the chronology of their composition. But criteria of internal association also influenced the compilation of poems in cycles in "Manuscript 1944/45," some of which have been given titles like "Der Sandmann" (The Sandman), "Vor Mitternacht" (Before Midnight), and "Blumen" (Flowers).

The "Typescript 1944" begins with the poem "Whence," which appears third in "Manuscript 1944/45" as "In the Park." This poem reads:

Nacht. Und alles ist da:	Night. And everything is here:
der See, die Bäume, der Kahn;	the lake, the trees, the boat;
. . .	. . .
Der einzige Schwan kommt vorüber.	The only swan crosses over.
Wie, wenn ein zitternder Stern	What, if a trembling star
. . .	. . .
. . . fiel in den See?	. . . were to fall into the lake?
. . .	. . .
Ob das Rotkehlchen stürbe?	If the robin would die?

Czernowitz did not have a lake with a swan. Presumably Celan was inspired by the Cişmigiu park in Bucharest, where swans did in fact swim in an artificial pond. The style of this poem's language does not yet show Rilke's influence and thus further confirms the assumption that young Celan wrote it on his first visit to Bucharest. This visit took place in the fall of 1933, when Paul Antschel had not yet turned fourteen.

There Was a Freedom

Two other poems are presumably very early ones. The poem "Wunsch" (Wish), which opens the "Manuscript 1944/45" and is also in the "Typescript 1944," reads:

Es krümmen sich Wurzeln.	Roots writhe.
Darunter	Underneath
wohnt wohl ein Maulwurf..	a mole seems to live..
oder ein Zwerg...	or a dwarf...
oder nur Erde	or just earth
und ein silberner Wasser-	and a silver strip of water
streifen...	
Besser	Better were it
wär Blut.	blood.

And the poem "Legende" (Legend), which only appears in the typescripts, ends with the following lines:

Löse ich, lösest du	Do I solve, do you solve
das rostige Rätsel der Erde	the rusty riddle of the earth
mit blutigem Spatenstich?	with a bloody cut of the spade?

Common to the three poems are the themes of "blood" and "death," as well as the questioning voice. Perhaps the phrase "the rusty riddle" in the poem "Legend" provides a clue to all three poems. Struggling with the typical problems of puberty, the young author might have faced difficult riddles, and the repetitive use of the words "blood," "red," and "rusty" could in fact refer to the feminine element he found very mysterious. The puberty noticeable in the background here speaks with some certainty for the early composition of these poems.

Paul Celan

If one compares the three poems "Whence," "Wish," and "Legend" with the beginning of the Mother's Day poem of 1938, which Celan wrote at seventeen, it becomes clear to what extent Paul's poetic expression grew from his close reading of Rilke's work:

> Kein ankerloses Tasten stört die Hand
> und nachts verstreutes Heimweh trägt die Not
> gefalteter Gebete zitternd hin vors Rot
> im Bangen deiner Züge, dunkeler gespannt.

> No anchorless groping disturbs the hand
> and at night, scattered nostalgia bears the need
> for folded prayers trembling before the red
> of your anguished features, more darkly taut.

And the last line of the poem reads: "Because you are peace, Mother, a glimmer from out of the ground."

It is worth mentioning that two poems which appear in both "Typescript 1944" and "Manuscript 1944/45" were known to two of Paul's female friends in the thirties. One of them was never published* and, untitled, begins with the words: "Out of that glance you often deny me." The second stanza reads:

> Als ich dich seltsam überflog
> behieltest du das Rauschen meiner Schwinge?
> Und als ich mich zu dir hinüberbog,
> war ich es oder wars die Nebelschlinge?

*Now published, 1989, in *Das Frühwerk*, ed. Barbara Wiedemann, Suhrkamp, p. 81. —M. B.

There Was a Freedom

When I flew over you strangely
did you keep the rush of my wings?
And when I leaned over toward you,
was it I or was it the trap of the fog?

The poem reflects the questionable nature, still remembered by the women after many years, of their relationship with Paul. The second poem is the one called "Drüben" (Over There), reprinted in *Der Sand aus den Urnen*, which was known to the girls without a title, which Paul only added upon publication. It begins with the line, "Only beyond the chestnut trees lies the world." Paul's girlfriends knew the streets lined with chestnut trees and they knew the poem—they had never seen the volume *Der Sand aus den Urnen*.[96]

In his last year at the Gymnasium, Paul read Nietzsche's *Thus Spoke Zarathustra* and *Beyond Good and Evil*. He told his friends how much these books impressed him. This led to his being nicknamed "Superman,"[97] which did not seem to have bothered him much, since "Paul always stood above things and the people surrounding him."[98]

In June of 1938 Paul took his graduation exam. In keeping with Austrian habits, it was still referred to as the "Matura," but was officially called "Bacalaureat," and was administered according to the French method, whereby none of the student's teachers could be a member of the examination board, which was headed by a university professor. The examiners were particularly strict and everything but impartial toward Jewish students, so that, in Czernowitz, the final mark assigned to Jews was rarely above average, whereas in Bucharest or in the old Romanian provinces, where the Jews presented relatively few graduation candidates, such a strict exam was very unusual. Paul received only 6.65 points out of 10, a result barely above the passing minimum of six points.[99] He remained indifferent, however, since he was above all happy to have put school behind him.

Paul and his parents agreed that he should continue his studies. Even the subject of study was already decided, at least for the parents. He was to become a doctor, which for a Romanian Jew was still the position with the best prospects. Paul hesitated for a short time, since according to his interests he would have preferred the natural sciences, perhaps botany. As he later told friends, medical studies also tempted him, because he saw in them a way "to learn more about the human being" and "to be able to help people."[100] So after a short reflection, Paul agreed to study medicine.[101]

German and Austrian universities were out of the question given the current political situation. Most Romanian Jews therefore went to France for their studies, where the Romanian Bacalaureat was academically equivalent to the French Baccalauréat and where one could receive a diploma that made it also possible to practice the profession in France. The first, preparatory year of university studies was usually completed in one of the provinces and only then did students enter one of the large universities in Paris or Strasbourg. Paul, Manuel, and several other Czernowitz graduates chose Tours. There was the École préparatoire de médicine, which was in fact not an actual medical school, but rather an institution for the first year of medical studies offering instruction only in the "P. C. N."subjects: physics, chemistry, and natural sciences. In addition, in this inexpensive provincial city one could be sure to get by on a low monthly allowance.

Suddenly and unexpectedly, however, Paul's father objected to his plan of beginning his studies right away. He spoke of certain prospects of obtaining an immigration visa for a South American country, but only considered it possible to come up with the money for emigration if Paul temporarily postponed his studies. Paul did not take his father's objections seriously, because he did not recognize the need to emigrate—especially not to "uncivilized" South America—and since his mother left the choice up to him, the decision that Paul should study in Tours was final.[102]

His departure date was set for the beginning of November, although the school year in Tours did not begin until the end of the month. This was because Paul was to make the trip via London, where his aunt Berta had been living for several months since her escape from Vienna following the German annexation of Austria. The family in Czernowitz thus hoped to receive an unvarnished report about their relative's well-being, and Paul on the other hand agreed to the detour in the hope of attending Shakespeare plays and because Manuel also wanted to travel via London. Of the two routes to London, the longer crossed Yugoslavia and Italy, the shorter led across sovereign German territory. This did not present a problem, since at that time Romanian Jews could still obtain German entry and transit visas without any difficulty, and getting to know Germany surely interested Paul, as one of his friends has confirmed.[103] At the last moment, however, it turned out that, because of a mistake made by the travel agency, only Manuel was able to follow the original travel plan, and Paul had to depart at a later date. Thus he undertook his first big voyage on his own.

On the morning of November 9, 1938, Paul boarded the express train that was to take him first to Berlin. On that day he travelled through Poland and, from Cracow, reached the

Paul Celan

German border in the early evening. At twilight he was crossing moorland, a landscape unknown to Paul, the memory of which was to be recalled in a poem:

> Es steht gekrümmt ein Birkenstamm:
> gekrümmte weisse Kreide.
> Drei Wolken links. Ein Bergeskamm.
> Und Heide, Heide, Heide.
> . . .

> Gnarled stands the birch-trunk:
> gnarled white chalk.
> Three clouds to the left. A mountain crest.
> And moors, moors, moors.
> . . .[104]

Paul describes the landscape in four stanzas, but two questions arise at the end of the poem: "Who might consolingly utter dreams here?" and "Do the winds slumber here?"

Strangely, this poem is reminiscent of a Yiddish folk song which Celan surely knew as did all Czernowitz Jews. It begins:

> Mid-way stands a tree
> That bends into itself.
> A Jew travels to the Land of Israel
> His eyes are swollen with tears.

The second and last stanza ends with the following lines:

> When we travel to the Land of Israel,
> There will be great joy.[105]

There Was a Freedom

Not only the image of the tree standing bent and crooked, but also the hope of that voyage to freedom, which promises the "Land of Israel," could support the assumption that Celan's memory of the Yiddish folk song fused with his thoughts on his trip through Nazi Germany, giving rise to the poem "While Travelling." The biographical background, at least, indicates it. Celan had, after all, wrung the permission to study in France from his father—who had actually wanted to emigrate to Palestine, but then agreed, in the face of the growing dangers in Romania, to the temporary solution of emigrating sooner to South America—with the help of his mother. In the process he had ridiculed his father's fears. But during the lonely trip through the German moorland, he must have had time and leisure enough to think about whether he was right in dismissing his father's worries about the future. On this trip he must certainly have begun to realize that Nazi Germany no longer represented that culture which he had hoped to find. His possible questions, however, about whether those Jews who, like his father, wanted to go to Palestine were in fact justified, may have given rise to the question with which the poem closes: was this Germany still a place where dreams and slumber could offer consolation?

Paul's incipient questions were gruesomely answered in Berlin. For years he told no one of what he had experienced there. Not until the volume *Die Niemandsrose* did he speak of it in poetic terms:

> . . .
>
> über Krakau
> bist du gekommen, am Anhalter
> Bahnhof
> floss deinen Blicken ein Rauch zu,
> der war schon von morgen. . . .

Paul Celan

•

. . .
via Cracow
you came, at the Anhalter
train station
smoke floated to your eyes,
it was already the morrow's. . . . [106]

Paul arrived in Berlin the day after *Kristallnacht*.

Without stopping, he then crossed Germany and reached Paris by way of Belgium. He postponed the trip to England until his next vacation. [107]

VI

Memory of France

Du denk mit mir: der Himmel von Paris, die grosse Herbstzeitlose . . .

Together with me recall: the sky of Paris, that giant autumn crocus . . .

U NDER a cloudy November sky, shortly before his
eighteenth year, Paul first saw Paris. Here—in this international city, whose sky reflected the pale colors of the autumn
sun—he wanted to spend his free days until the beginning of
the academic year in Tours. Leonid Miller was the main
speaker at the illegal meeting of the Anti-Fascist Youth in the
summer of 1935 in the Cecina Forest and had met Paul there.
He now studied medicine in Paris and had invited Paul to stay
with him. He was also expected by Bruno Schrager, his
mother's brother, who lived in the rue de l'École. [108]
Paul roamed the Latin Quarter with Leonid, strolled in
the Luxembourg Gardens, and tried to take up with young
Parisian girls, with whom he had no success despite his elegant
French. Bruno led him through the night spots of Montmartre

95

and Montparnasse so that he could see the legendary Bohemian world for himself. He did not develop a taste for the nightlife, however—he tended much more towards the Louvre, the Rodin Museum, and especially the Comédie Française, of which he had dreamed for so long.

In Tours Manuel had already rented joint accommodations for them, but they only lived together for a short while. Paul's lifestyle was very different from Manuel's and so as not to disturb his friend he sought separate accommodations. But they continued to meet everyday at lectures and during laboratory work. Neither found his studies very stimulating, as they basically recapitulated the natural sciences they had studied at the Gymnasium, even if the laboratory work demanded more time. The teaching methods corresponded almost entirely with those of the Gymnasium, and they had to be promptly on time in the morning as their presence was strictly recorded. Academic freedom, as was common in Central European institutes of higher education, was unknown to the Tours École préparatoire de médecine. Paul's active mind then sought and found something better than spending his free afternoons and evenings poring over books. He initiated two friendships that were to stimulate his interests in very differing fields.

He told Manuel of his acquaintance with a French student, who lived in Tours but studied literature elsewhere, only spending weekends in his native city. Paul never mentioned his new friend's name; he spoke only of the "Trotskyite." Although Paul had intended even at home not to draw political attention to himself and certainly did not want to risk deportation from France for political activities, he was still tempted to learn about the Trotskyite movement, to which he was sympathetic. He had probably also been aware of the connection between the surrealists and Trotsky, indeed, André Breton and Trotsky met in 1938, and in the same year the "Féderation de l'art révolutionnaire indépendant" (Federation for Independent Revolutionary Art) was founded.[109] Paul did not speak of this. But he did mention invitations to meals at the home of his French friend—a rare honor for foreigners in France—and of encounters with Spanish immigrants, who impressed him very much. Paul spoke of folkloric events the Spaniards organized, of enthralling Fandango and Seguidilla dances and of guitar music. He hardly ever told Manuel of the refugees' war experiences or their misery. Among them, however, he might have learned of "Abadias," the "old man from Huesca," and heard his "Shepherd's Spanish."[110]

Life in the Catholic provincial city was relatively monotonous for foreign students, and not many of them managed to establish contact with the French as Paul had. It was not even easy to flirt with the girls, as they were strictly supervised. Thus Paul sought further acquaintances elsewhere. In the Society for German and French Rapprochement, founded by German immigrants, he finally made a second friend: Eliyahu Pinter. He was a German who had fled to Palestine in 1933, and had come from his new home to France for practical training in urban planning. They met several times a week in a café or for long evening walks, and their conversations centered on their common interest in literature. Pinter admired his friend's great sensitivity to poetic diction, but Paul never mentioned his own poetry. Pinter also found it astonishing that an East European Jew possessed such an extensive and sound body of knowledge. From his time in Germany he had kept the usual prejudices against East European Jews and was now forced to admit that he felt inferior to one of them.

During this time, Paul was reading the novels of Julien Green and the poetry of Charles Péguy. He also spoke often

Paul Celan

of André Gide and seemed to have been well-acquainted with his works. If the French "esprit" was mentioned, Paul would quote Montaigne, Pascal, and La Rochefoucauld. German writers such as Rilke, George, Heine, and Thomas Mann were analyzed and compared. And in a conversation about Shakespeare, Paul told his friend of his dissatisfaction with the renditions of the sonnets by Gundolf, George, and Kraus. In the case of Karl Kraus, he regretted that Kraus, in general, had too often wasted his linguistic ability on banal subjects.

Paul and Eliyahu also attended concerts performed by a local ensemble. There his friend noticed Paul's understanding of and sensitivity to music. They also met a violinist in the orchestra, a German immigrant who sometimes joined them in the café and entertained them with boasts about his love affairs. This acquaintance was a welcome distraction for both young men.

Although Paul had already passed himself off as a religiously indifferent Jew, Pinter managed to bring his friend to a Sabbath service in the Tours synagogue. The local rabbi had been born in Palestine, and when Pinter introduced Paul to him after the prayers, they were amazed to learn that Paul could participate in a conversation conducted in Hebrew. Afterward, the rabbi, who had a son of Paul's age, invited the young men to the Sabbath meal with his family.

Paul knew well how to avoid conflicts among his friends of different interests, and with some of them even left out entirely certain topics of conversation. He gave Pinter, with whom he never discussed politics or the Spanish immigrants, the impression of being an open-minded person capable of enthusiasm, who loved life, had a well-developed sense of humor and was rarely sentimental—except when he once spoke of the disappointments inflicted on him by an unknown French girl.

Memory of France

But during his stay in Tours, he did not forget his friends at home. Ilse Goldmann once received "a beautiful letter" from him, and he sent Gustav Chomed a series of detailed descriptions of the conditions in France, which he entitled "A Winter's Tale."

At Christmas Paul received a joyful surprise—his friend Erich Einhorn had come to Paris. So he once again postponed the long overdue trip to London, went to Paris and spent his vacation there in the company of Erich, Leonid Miller and Manuel Singer. But being together again with Erich was probably most important for Paul.

It was not until the Easter holidays that he made the trip across the Channel. The visit with his aunt Berta Antschel, who was very fond of Paul, was for him rather a formality. He was primarily happy that he was again able to meet friends: Yitzhak Alpan and Yancu Pesate, school friends from Czernowitz, were studying in England, and Manuel, having responded to invitations from relatives living there, was also in London at the time. Now Paul could finally see his beloved Shakespeare dramas performed by famous actors and visit the British Museum. In conversation with his friends he discussed such English classics as Milton and Thomas More. For the city itself, however, Paul never developed much of a fondness. To his aunt, who wanted to invite him for the summer vacation as well, he explained that only Paris was worthy of his love but that he had planned in any case to spend his semester break at home.

In July of 1939 Paul took the final examination of the first academic year and immediately returned to Czernowitz. His first year abroad was behind him, and he was satisfied, as he had learned much that was new, even if it was not exactly in the medical field.

VII

Cyrillics

(Kyrillisches, Freunde, auch das
ritt ich über die Seine
ritts übern Rhein.)

(Cyrillics, friends, that too
I rode across the Seine,
rode it across the Rhine.)

I N Czernowitz, in the summer of 1939, there was as yet little awareness of the impending war. Paul vacationed happily, meeting old friends again, often swimming in the Prut, hiking through the surrounding forests, and enjoying the beautiful summer weather.

The outbreak of the Second World War changed the prevailing conditions almost at a single stroke. The significance of the Hitler-Stalin pact, concluded in August of 1939,* was immediately recognized: since Romania could not expect any help from its Western allies, it was at the mercy of the despotism of Stalin and Hitler. An immediate threat came particularly

---

*The pact contained secret provisions for the future transfer to Soviet Russia of the three Baltic republics as well as the Romanian province of Bessarabia and northern Bukovina. —M.B.

Paul Celan

from Soviet Russia, which had never given up its claims to Bessarabia, the province lost to Romania in 1918. Because the Romanian army was mobilized on the eastern border for this reason and the reservists were also called up, the country's economy was severely handicapped, leading to unrest in the population, which had been living in a carefree manner.[111]

Paul, barely 19 years old, was not yet subject to military service, but a return to France had become impossible. In Czernowitz there was no medical school, and the quota for Jews that was in force at all Romanian universities rendered nearly every attempt to continue his studies in the country hopeless. Paul's university friends, who had also been taken by surprise during their vacation, could not continue their studies in France and sought temporary solutions in which they would not have to stray too far from medicine. Most of them enrolled in the natural sciences at Czernowitz University.

Paul, however, took a decisive turn. He enrolled in the department of Romance Languages and Literature in the school of philosophy—his "Memory of France" had its effect. He complained to his friends about having to interrupt his medical studies, and he spoke of continuing them after the war, and of perfecting his knowledge of the French language and literature in the meantime. It still seemed difficult for him to admit openly that his choice of this apparent interim solution in fact meant a final break with medicine. Paul may also have come to this decision earlier, as the year spent in France may presumably have made clear to him where his true interests lay.

Paul took his study of the Romance languages and literatures so seriously that he also studied Old French. Dissatisfied with the Romanian-French school books, he acquired Meyer-Lübke's *Handbuch der Romanistik (Handbook of Romance Studies)*, which provided him with the developments in this

Cyrillics

field as they were studied in German universities. Paul also turned to the problems of linguistics raised by Ferdinand de Saussure in his *Course in General Linguistics*. The linguist Chaim Ginniger, who met Paul during this time, speaks of this in a letter which he begins by asking whether one can do any justice at all to "such an *opaque* subject as Celan" for a formulaic explanation:

I noticed Paul mainly because of his precise use of language. I managed to read one or two of his poems through one of his girlfriends, and I was also delighted with their succinctness. It was for this reason that I introduced him to Rose Ausländer. Our discussions were first and foremost about the process of linguistic denotation, of language as application. He had learned from Saussure the distinction between "langue" and "parole." I also tended to call on him for that reason. He was very well-versed in linguistics. But it is more commonly known that he learned foreign languages very easily.

In a meadow in Gurahumora I got to know another side of Paul. I had the opportunity to hear how he was able to label flowers and plants and describe many of them very beautifully.

I would not be able to confirm that he expressed any interest in Yiddish literature. I am not at all convinced that he loved Steinbarg's fables. Perhaps I can claim that the detailed nature of the declarations, of the poetic manifestation in Steinbarg, seemed to run counter to him. In addition, I never heard him utter a Yiddish word.

Before his escape from Czernowitz he left me two handbooks of the Romance language scholar Meyer-Lubke. When I then made my remarks about them, I was astonished by the maturity of his linguistic opinions, which he expressed on that occasion.

I cannot speak of Celan's childhood, since I met him when he had returned from France as a medical student. The thicket must be very dark, if his mature years . . . bring so little to light.[112]

The university studies only partly satisfied Paul's intellect. He did not want to lose his orientation in the isolation brought about by the war. He wanted to know how humanity had been brought to the verge of self-destruction. This is why he was not content simply with newspaper and radio reports, but also began to read the political literature of the preceding years. He studied the articles in the *Weltbühne* of Jacobsohn, the writings of Kurt Tucholsky and also André Gide's *Return from the USSR*. In doing so, he realized that the opinions a few people had held and written down, and many of which had been decried only a few years earlier as false prophecy, had now become a gruesome reality. Paul was deeply disturbed.

Despite the war against Hitler's German Reich and despite Paul's seemingly definitive tendency toward Romance studies, German remained the language of his inner life and thus of his poems, which he "wrote in secret," as an early friend reported, because he "was even a little ashamed of writing poetry."[113] In this situation it was immensely comforting to read Gustav Landauer's lines: "Mein Deutschtum und mein Judentum tun sich nichts zuleid und vieles zulieb," ("My Germanness and my Jewishness are not at all antagonistic but remain very friendly"). Not until many years later would Celan doubt the validity of this sentence, but in the first winter of war it still seemed to offer him a life-line.[114]

The social life of the young people around Paul was centered, in 1938 and 1939, in the home of the Alper family. Two brothers, a sister, and their mother held an unusual appeal. The secret was simplicity and freedom. The children's father, a very active businessman who spent most of his time away from home, allowed his family to do as they saw fit, and every visitor felt completely at home there. There was a constant coming and going—the house door was always unlocked, even when no member of the family was present—and guests could do as they pleased. They were frank in their conversations, and if someone needed advice or encouragement, Mrs. Alper provided help with tact and understanding. Paul proved to be particularly devoted to them.[115]

At the university, Paul surrounded himself with a second circle, which overlapped only marginally with that of the Alper home. In his class the girls were in the majority, since literature studies were already very popular with them. They all competed for Paul's friendship, but he became even more demanding in what concerned their external appearance and their intellectual abilities.

Paul's fellow student Dorothea Müller-Altneu reported the following about this period of their studies:

Paul belonged to our group and we were proud of him. When a young girl who had chosen a different field of study pitied us because we were mostly female and because the many strapping boys of her group didn't belong to ours, she received from our quietest and most childish colleague the unexpected reply: 'But you don't have Paul.' . . . Those who knew this twenty-year-old will not be able to forget his oval, cameo-like face. It is strange that his infinitely rich and emotional inner life was never mirrored in his features. His delicate nostrils did not quiver, his eyebrows were not drawn together, the clear forehead remained free of wrinkles. His face was inscrutable. It was a face that wanted to reveal nothing, exposed nothing of the cryptic depths of his poetic soul.

No close friend knew much about his inner life. Only in his poetry was the wide stream of experience allowed to gush forth.

When I think about young Paul . . ., it becomes clear to me that not one facet of his personality fits into any cliché.

He rejected the purposeful exterior carelessness of the Bohemian, which other young artists regarded as a sign of their identity and uniqueness. He was . . . of a spotless, discreet, relaxed elegance. I remember a whole series of colorful sweaters and vests into which a caring mother's hands had knitted love and beauty. . . . Paul was not indulgent. His judgment—whether it dealt with teachers or colleagues—was severe and mercilessly just . . . His uncompromising judgment even seemed unfair at times to us young people. Today I know for sure that Paul was never mistaken. . . . He despised everything amateurish. . . . He was also blessed with the same divining faculty of judgment in the evaluation of the truly good. It was the quiet, modest ones, who did not stand out through any kind of posing, that he kindly and truly appreciated. . . . He made the heaviest demands on himself, however. He required the best of himself.

As a first-year student . . . it was believed that his pure, fluent French was his mother tongue. . . . He loved praise; he found the inability to answer unbearable. An exam passed with distinction could release in him a storm of unrestrained joy, which often appeared childish.[116]

Cyrillics

•

On New Year's Eve, 1939, several friends sat together without girls at Konrad Deligdisch's parents' home. As usual Paul was the center of the conversation. Yitzhak Alpan remembers very well—it was his farewell evening; a few weeks later he emigrated to Palestine:

We drank moderately, but discussed all the more heartily. We spoke about political writers. Paul raved about Kurt Tucholsky and spoke against Karl Kraus, whom he disliked. If it had to be mockery and irony, then he preferred the writings of Villon or Christian Morgenstern.

This evening's conversation was no different from others: one had the feeling that Paul wanted to speak *to* people, rather than *with* them.

We then sang songs together: songs that expressed the romantic longing of middle-class youths for political changes, especially those that recalled the courageous struggle of the Spanish Republicans. We hoped—on the threshold of the second year of war—that a better and more just world order was possible and nearby.[117]

This hope did not seem unjustified in neutral Romania. Even the Romanian government had apparently not taken the mobilization of the army very seriously and had sent its soldiers home on vacation for the winter.

In the spring of 1940—the academic year at the university was coming to an end and the students were preparing for exams—that which was most feared happened: the Soviet Union demanded that the Romanian government evacuate immediately and unconditionally Bessarabia and northern Bukovina, including Czernowitz. Since Hitler's armies had already occupied vast parts of France and now threatened England, Romania could not count on help from the Western powers and so gave up the two provinces, which had been part of the kingdom since 1918.

The Jewish students could not believe their eyes when their Romanian colleagues and lecturers followed the example of the majority of the city's population and fled head over heels. A few rifleshots rang out on the Austria-Platz and then— silence! Suddenly the rumbling of armored tanks was heard: the Red Army moved into the city abandoned by the Romanians. It was June 28, 1940.

The university closed its gates. Idle as they now were, the students strolled through the streets and tried to make conversation with Soviet soldiers. Although it was difficult to be understood in the local Ukrainian dialect, they were able, in the end, to make contact with members of the Red Army, whose leisurely speech and jovial farmers' faces inspired confidence. From their mouths came—like a well-learned lesson—always the same thing: "We have freed you from capitalism and fascism; now you will get to know the Soviet worker and farmer paradise!"

But the leisure of walks and conversation did not last long. The occupying authorities asked the young people to become volunteers with whom they hoped to facilitate peaceful contacts with the population. Several of Paul's friends signed on immediately. He hesitated at first, then allowed himself to be persuaded that they should respond to the good intentions of the new occupying authorities. He thus became an interpreter for a housing commission which was to arrange apartments for Soviet officers. Communication turned out not to be as difficult as it had seemed at first, but explaining to the affected civilians the "justice" of the billeting measures was an extremely thankless task. To Paul's relief, this volunteer service lasted only a few days.[118]

The summer of 1940 was sunny and warm. The young people used their vacation to swim in the river and to take walks, which to their dismay were restricted to the city parks, as the Soviet high command had prohibited excursions outside the city. On the few days of rainy weather, they sat in the Schwarze Adler, which had already become a popular "red" café, and drank coffee despite its rapidly declining quality. But their conversations and their observations of the Soviet people were more important than the refreshments that were served.

In September the university was reopened and began its "third existence:" the original German university had been turned into a Romanian one in 1918, and now it became Ukrainian. The majority of the faculty were Russians who had been called in from the interior of the Union, and a few were local teachers, who were not even qualified to teach at university level. "High school teachers had been raised overnight to the rank of professors and lecturers."[119] The only important criterion was fluency in Russian or Ukrainian. This knowledge was naturally now also required of the students. For this reason, Paul had already begun to study Russian during the vacation, and while the others were still "deciphering the spelling of Russian texts, he was reading Tolstoy's *War and Peace* in the original."[120]

In the Bukovina, the young academics now received the same salary given to university students in the Soviet Union, which corresponded to the pay of a regular worker. Paul was satisfied with this arrangement, since he possessed an income high enough even to support his parents. His father had been forced to give up his brokering business—as a "parasite" he might have been deported to a distant region of the USSR for "reproductivization"—and he now performed a subordinate function in the Planning and Building Control Office. His engineering diploma, received decades ago, was finally put to good use.

At the university, standards had now become frighteningly low. Romance studies, for instance, were conducted by a former Latin teacher from the girls' school. That she was a Czernowitz Jew could not even console the Jewish students for her incompetence. On the contrary: Paul was the first to begin to grumble and then to initiate and lead a rebellion. The students elected a delegation that was to complain to the dean—they hoped in this way to obtain a replacement for the Romance chair. Paul, as head of the delegation, however, received a stern rebuke from the dean. The place for rebellious enemies of the Soviet Union was Siberia. Paul was appalled and stammered that he was no enemy of the proletarian regime and, in fact, had collected donations for the "Red Help" as early as 1936. The Russian's face, however, revealed that he had heard nothing at all of the "Red Help." The students' action failed and its leaders were let off lightly with a strong reprimand and a warning not to engage again in such "unproletarian" activities. In Soviet terms, the case should have been brought up before the university's labor union, which was of course dominated by Communist leaders and would not have undertaken any action against "comrade Dean."

Paul no longer took the French lecturer seriously. He even permitted himself to hand the "baffled university-assistant" a letter which began with the words "My dear Brutus," instead of the required seminar paper. Bad consequences, however, did not follow this prank of Paul's.[121]

A short while later, the student David Seidmann, whom Paul had not gotten to know or begun to appreciate until this

academic year, was summoned to face the university's "Poli-
truk." He had been anonymously accused of concealing a
Zionist past and of still engaging in Zionist propaganda. When
his companions learned of the accusation, it was Paul who
passed the word that it was necessary "to protect their colleague
at any price from deportation to Siberia," which was the expected punishment. Called on as witnesses, the students could
in fact tell only the truth: they hadn't known Seidmann earlier,
but had also never heard of any Zionist activities on his part.
Seidmann stayed and these new Soviet citizens learned something from the authorities' approach and the means of reacting
to it. Paul's circle, meanwhile, had become one friend
richer.[122]

The teaching methods at the Soviet university were un-
pleasant in other ways as well. Day after day students had to
sit through eight hours of instruction, of which a specific part
was dedicated to the recapitulation of the daily curriculum.
Marxism-Leninism and the history of the Russian Communist
Party were part of the obligatory subjects for students in all
disciplines. The students of the "literary department" were also
required to study the history of Russian literature. In this subject, however, they had their only friendly professor, a young
Russian who claimed to be of aristocratic descent but had
converted to communism.[123] Whether he was an informer of
the NKVD, the state secret police, who was supposed to sniff
around the students' private lives, or truly the friend he pre-
tended to be, was never made clear. The fact remained that
this universiy professor, a quick-witted man, mingled among
the students, called them by their first names and joined them
in the café and on their walks through the city gardens. He
joked and sang like one of them. Dorothea Müller-Altneu said
of this time: "We had a new fatherland in which—as in the

song—the heart of man beats so freely. We sang the song and believed for a while in its pretty words. How this freedom was destined to be plagued we wouldn't find out until later. . ."[124]

In the following winter, dissatisfaction with the university alone no longer elicited sharp criticism of the Soviet regime from Paul and his friends. The general weaknesses of the system became increasingly clear. Complaints about the shortage of many goods essential to survival were faced with empty promises on the part of those responsible, and the feigned innocence of high functionaries concealed corruption and limitless egotism that shied away from no crime if it were profitable. The dissatisfaction now spread even to former communist sympathizers, even to old Party members, who in the capitalist era had been willing to go to jail for their convictions.

The students tried, through humor and clowning, to overcome the difficult situation. Paul was in his element. He now could be heard "laughing loudly and heartily" when he cheered up his university colleagues with his "live 'Punch-and-Judy Show,'" or when he "effortlessly performed the pirouette of a prima ballerina in a mock-gracious manner." He was also capable of "imitating half a dozen German dialects with dramatic perfection." His audience couldn't stop laughing.[125]

Despite his activities with his companions at the university, Paul did not forget his old friends, who had gone to work after the Gymnasium. Gustav Chomed, for instance, had been forced by the early death of his father to take a job as a bookkeeper and was occupied in the daytime. Nonetheless, he spent many evenings talking with Paul, who, since his return from France, was seeing to his friend's continued education. Since it was necessary now to learn Russian, Paul gave Gustav lessons and brought him to the point where he was able to read and understand Sergei Esenin's poems, which Paul was already trying to translate into German.[126]

While the anniversary of the October Revolution had passed relatively quietly, the first of May, 1941, was celebrated by the Soviet rulers with all the means available for their own proletarian-byzantine display of pomp and power. The students, like the workers and the functionaries, had to march in formation carrying gigantic portraits of Stalin, Lenin, or perhaps only Mikoyan. They swung banners carrying mottos like "Workers of the World, Unite!" and "Long live our genius comrade Stalin, father of all peoples!" In front of the platform on which the party bosses stood, they had to yell with increasingly sore throats, "Long live the great man Stalin!" or "Long live the invincible Soviet Union!," while the military band played deafening marches. Paul marched along, sad and disgusted. Much of what he experienced during his youth reappears in Paul's later poetry in a different form—and perhaps it is to the memory of this first of May that he refers in a poem from *Atemwende:*

DUNSTBÄNDER-, SPRUCHBÄNDER-AUFSTAND,
röter als rot,
. . . vor
Robbenvölkern.

UPRISING OF SMOKE BANNERS, WORD BANNERS,
redder than red
. . . in front of
seal peoples.[127]

VIII

The Glow of Berenice's Hair

Mein Herz strahlt wild vom herrlichen Bescheid.
Dein Haar vom Glanz aus Berenikes Haar.

My heart beams wildly from the marvelous tidings.
Your hair from the glow of Berenice's hair.

IN the eventful summer of 1940 Paul made an acquaintance that was to have a decisive impact on his life.[128] In the Alper home, the meeting place of idealistic young people, he met Ruth Lackner. This coincidental encounter led to a relationship which, in Paul's own words, required the "most intense commitment" from him and became the leading theme of his early poetry written between 1940 and 1945.[129]

Ruth Lackner was a graduate of the Bucharest School of Drama and was making her debut in Czernowitz at the Yiddish State Theater, which had been reopened by the Soviets. Her choice of this stage was no accident as she had been given a bilingual, German-Yiddish upbringing in Czernowitz. Ruth's father, a musical man, had distinguished himself early on as an ardent fighter for the Yiddish language—during his Ger-

Paul Celan

manistic studies in Czernowitz and then as lecturer at a Czernowitz state Gymnasium under the Habsburg Monarchy—and
he had later encouraged his daughter's wish to become an
actress. Even in her childhood he had allowed her to act in a
Yiddish children's theater, founded by a close friend of his,
the writer Eliezer Steinbarg. But what Ruth now experienced
as Yiddish theater in the Soviet era was, because of its low
standards, a great disappointment.

A few years older than Paul, Ruth had married early, but
was separated from her husband and now lived again with her
parents. After the evenings at the Alpers' a "dreamy and exult-
ant" Paul always accompanied the young actress home. Ruth
Lackner reports the following about her impression of Paul in
this circle:

> Although entirely unconventional in his social relations
> and friendships, Paul was very sensitive and easily hurt.
> A single inappropriate or stupid remark from someone in
> the social circle would silence Paul for a whole, long
> evening or even lead him to disappear quietly. No one
> would have dared, in any case, a direct attack on his
> person, since he was always the superior one.
>
> Paul despised presumption, half-hearted attitudes,
> and superficiality. He made the toughest demands espe-
> cially on himself, but he also imposed his imperative
> standards on the people around him. One got the impres-
> sion, even then, that he was not prepared to accept com-
> promises, that he strove exclusively for the absolute. This
> is why he came across as a tough, strict person to some
> of his acquaintances. Those who knew him more closely,
> however, knew that this toughness served as a protective
> shield, to keep the banal at a distance. In truth he was a

kind, helpful person, and this became evident in hard times. Despite all his eloquence, he was often so overcome with feelings that he would very suddenly become silent and take his leave, only to say later, in a short letter personally delivered, what he had been unable to express earlier.[130]

During the nightly walks home with Ruth, who shared many of his interests, Paul continued the discussions about writers and books begun in the larger circle. Rilke was still Paul's revered model, but he also felt attracted to Trakl's poetry and that of Klabund, in particular the latter's free renditions of Chinese verse. Among the older German poets he loved mainly Mörike, Novalis, and Hölderlin. His choice of prose writers included Fontane, Jean Paul, Kafka, and Thomas Mann, whose *Magic Mountain* provided the inspiration for his own poem "Bergfrühling" (Mountain Springtime).[130a] Since his stay in France, Paul had turned increasingly to Villon, Rimbaud, and Verlaine. Proust, Rolland, and Céline also impressed him. Of English-language authors he knew James Joyce from German translations, but had diligently struggled through Shakespeare's works in the original. Among the Russian writers, Sergei Esenin and Vladimir Mayakovsky had recently fascinated him, and he knew Dostoevsky, Gogol, and Gorky from German translations.

As before, Paul loved the fairy tales that had filled his childhood, and he read with great interest the collections of the Grimm Brothers and the tales of Wilhelm Hauff, Hans Christian Andersen, and Oscar Wilde. His reading of *A Thousand and One Nights* resulted in the poem "Sindbad," and the poem "Die Schneekönigin" (The Snow Queen) also has something of a fairy tale tone:

Paul Celan

•

Der Königinnen mildeste im Schnee hier
entsinnt sich nicht des Spiegleins, das zersprang.
Und gleicht dein Aug auch jenem grünen Seetier:
sie hört dich an nur eine Stunde lang.

The mildest of the queens here in the snow
does not recall the little mirror that broke.
And if your eye also resembles that green sea-creature:
she listens to you only for an hour. [131]

Although Paul enjoyed talking with Ruth about the theater
and playwrights, he displayed only passing interest in the Yiddish stage on which she performed. He attended a few of its
performances, but the Yiddish folk-plays and the Soviet propaganda plays, badly translated from Russian and performed by
mediocre actors, all bored him. It was not the actress in Ruth
that attracted Paul, and he did not like to see her in those
surroundings. For her, however, the theater offered the only
possibility of practicing her profession under Soviet rule. Paul,
on the other hand, had seen good theater in Paris and London:
the Comédie Française and the English Shakespeare performances were a vivid memory that now yearned for an equivalent.

Paul much preferred to visit the Ukrainian City Theater,
whose performances were given in the building of the former
German, and later Romanian, City Theater. There he was
delighted with the involuntarily comic effect produced by the
representation of famous classical tragedies by miserable actors.
With extremely lively mimicry he later reenacted their exag-
gerated gestures and ridiculous intonation.

With growing confidence Paul and Ruth began to exchange childhood memories. Ruth told of Graz, her birthplace,

and her first impressions of life gathered there and thus reawakened in Paul his earlier pictures of the "magical city, Vienna." As a child he had even convinced himself for a time that he was born in Vienna and had proudly shared this "secret" with his little friends.

When Ruth mentioned Steinbarg's children's theater and quoted a few verses from the poet's fables, the story resurfaced in Paul's memory of "Rabbi Leiserl, who talked to himself, and questioned his melancholy: / What is one? / Then he heard the fly buzz, that was pestering him: / 'But one is none!'" Paul loved this poem and considered it Steinbarg's best—it was for him the expression of a deep philosophy of life, and he often recited these Yiddish verses to himself.[132]

Apart from these verses, however, one never heard him quote anything in Yiddish. He considered this language "corrupt German," and regarded, for instance, the local Yiddish poet Itzik Manger, who would later enjoy international fame in America and elsewhere, not as a real poet but rather a phenomenon of folklore.[133] Still, Paul was tolerant enough not to pick a quarrel with outspoken proponents of Yiddish.

Paul's attitude toward the different languages that were spoken in Czernowitz or printed in the books and daily newspapers was often the topic of his discussions with Ruth. Again and again Paul emphasized that, despite his advanced knowledge of several foreign languages and his ability to learn new ones easily, he would never write poems in any but his mother tongue.

Ruth's parents like to see Paul in their home and became good friends with him. Paul was in especially good standing with Ruth's mother. Since the older woman loved to be told stories, Paul invented fantastic tales which he passed off as true occurrences. And Ruth's mother was always surprised anew to find out that the stories were Paul's inventions. In his absence she called him the "prince"—perhaps she was thinking of a Prince Charming . . .

Ruth's father allowed Paul to participate in his circle of friends who gathered nearly every evening in his home. Among them was also a junior high school teacher whom Paul knew from Czernowitz University: Chaim Ginniger. He now continued with him their previously begun conversations about linguistic problems. The other guests of the house were all Yiddish scholars like Ruth's father, and they taught, as he now did, at the Yiddish State School. Like all Soviet schools, it covered ten grades and encompassed primary as well as secondary education.

At Ruth's parents' home Paul also encountered the reciter Lewin, whose Yiddish readings stimulated him to reflect on the art of the word and his own manner of reciting poetry. Paul remained friends with Lewin for many years. Another constant guest in the house was Hersh Segal, a mathematics teacher at the Yiddish School and an enthusiast of art and literature. Before the war, he had published, on his own or in association with others, several collections of Yiddish and German poems as well as art portfolios of Jewish painters. His published collection of Yiddish folksongs, supplemented by their melodies, had awakened particular interest in his friends for Jewish folk art. Segal liked to steer conversations in the direction of those subjects of which he was particularly fond.[134]

What no one could allow himself to talk about except in the most confidential circles—the most unsettling problems of the day, the war in Europe and the Soviet regime—was possible among Ruth's father's friends. The Soviet press and the state radio provided only very summary accounts of the war. The glorification of the government and its leading personalities with Stalin at the peak, on the other hand, was much more verbose. In both the press and on the radio there was also extensive talk of the maximum commitment that every Soviet citizen had to make for the economic prosperity of the Soviet Union. The inhabitants of Czernowitz, however, quickly saw through the falseness and corruption of Stalinism. In circles of family and friends there was only incisive criticism and complaint. The Soviet Union was praised, however, for knowing well enough to stay out of the European war—even if at the price of a pact with Hitler.

When Ruth visited Paul's house, which occurred much less frequently, she was received with the same friendliness that Paul's mother imparted to all of his friends. As in Paul's school days, the Antschel home was a gathering place for young people, whom his mother liked to join when her housework permitted. It was not rare for her to participate in the discussions and to astonish Paul's friends with her great understanding for the views of the young. As the schoolmates who visited Paul earlier had seen, it became clear to Ruth why Paul never referred to her in any terms other than as his "beloved mother," and she recognized his adoration and worship in the glances he exchanged with his mother.

The relationship between Paul and Ruth became more intense as they longed to spend more time together, away from family and friends. Evening after evening Paul waited at the stage door of the theater to accompany Ruth home. As the actual path home would have been very short, Paul made detours through the city's gardens all the way to the remote Habsburgshöhe or into the windy Flurgasse behind the Volksgarten.

There, according to Ruth, they sauntered side by side in a leisurely fashion. Paul, slim and light, with a dancer's gait, as it were, and Ruth, delicate and petite, trying to keep up with her friend. Sometimes Paul stopped in front of an old tree, felt the trunk, the gnarled bark, a twig, or a leaf, and astonished his girlfriend by giving its German and Latin names and, leaning against the tree, speaking of the classification of plants, their needs for survival, and their propagation. Then he was able suddenly to resume his way and abandon himself again to the quiet observation of the flowers and bushes in the moonlight, gently stoking a plant here and breaking off a flower or a leaf there.

Once, Paul tore a handful of weeds out of the lawn, held it in his outstretched right hand high above, toward the stars, and yelled: "Weeds, you stalks of the stars!" That same night he wrote a poem, in which he used this spontaneously found line. To this German poem, however, he gave—as he sometimes also did in later years—a French title: "Les Adieux."[135]

In the mornings, flowers were often delivered to Ruth's home: tulips or roses, carnations or daisies—flowers that Paul loved. If there were no flowers to buy, Paul knew where to pick them. Whenever Ruth saw him, he had a flower or a blossoming twig in his hand. Hidden among the flowers was usually a letter, with a poem of Paul's. Night after night he wrote poems that were all meant for his beloved woman.

Paul rapidly immersed himself in a dreamworld, in which there was only room for love and poetry. Rilke's sentence fit: "Life, then, is only the dream of a dream, but wakefulness is elsewhere."[136]

For Paul this was a period of rich poetic creation. In the poems, whose tone is tinged with traditional romanticism, yet remains individual, love is initially defined by metaphors. It is not until later that the poems contain more direct statements as well. But the dreamlike blurring of love and nature prevails.

The Glow of Berenice's Hair

He wrote in an untitled poem that begins with the words "Quiet, beloved, quiet:"

. . .

Die knospenden Finger des Abends
greifen den goldenen Gesang
in den Harfen der Sträucher.

. . .

. . .

The budding fingers of evening
pluck the golden song
on the bushes' harps.

. . .

And in the poem "Schlaflied" (Lullaby), the first stanza runs:

Mit den Faltern, mit der Nacht
lass mich ein in deinen Schlummer:
über dir bin ich ein stummer
Atemzug der wacht,

With the butterflies, with the night
let me into your slumber:
above you I am a speechless
breath that wakes,[137]

Love, as revealed in Celan's poetry of these years, is experienced as something infinitely delicate, that can barely bear to be touched. So he says to the beloved in one of the poems: "The moon / . . . draws your picture in the hollows. . . ." In another he writes: "I easily inflict an aching on you: / you may only float and you may be drunk." In the closing lines of a third poem his emotional relationship is finally expressed with restraint: "In the changing nights / I ache from you to you." The beloved is in essence the "silent, lovely, light one" and for the loving one "the days' consolation."[138]

Paul was aware of his dreamlike state. He calls, for example, to the beloved in a poem: "Princess Tireless, come along: / keep pace with my dreams today!"[139] And so she does: for years she was to follow him into his dreamworld, and the poetry echoed her paces.

Nature, as described in his poems, the flowers and plants that Paul knew as none of his friends did, is the basis for the poetic shaping of his love and also reflects its transformations: "No longer as once and before / you were here the sloe now blooms." On another occasion he addresses the beloved:

. . .
Du musst der Pracht des Gartenmohns vertrauen,
der stolz verschwendet, was der Sommer bot;
und lebt, dass er am Boden deiner Brauen
errät, ob deine Seele träumt im Rot...
. . .

. . .
You must trust the splendor of the garden poppy,
which proudly squanders what the summer offered;
and lives to guess by the arch of your
brow, whether your soul dreams in red...
. . .

Other poems develop this flower imagery, which is meaningful to the lovers: tulips appear as "shining stars," the "wood anemones that tremble of evening, / bloom, glimmering, before our darkness," the autumn crocus *(Herbstzeitlose)* becomes, as in Novalis, the "Zeitlosen," (Timeless ones) that take a "breath" for "a thousand autumns," and "bubbling sleep" is bestowed on the "darkest pair, to the left of a floating carnation."[140]

Most characteristic of young Celan's interweaving of life and dream, of dream and poetry, is the poem "Sternenlied" (Stars' Song). The first stanza reads:

Nichts kann, das sich im Mondschein noch begibt,
je sein wie damals, als der grosse Wagen
uns tönend aufnahm. Keinen den er liebt
wird er, wie einst uns zwei, begeistert tragen.

Nothing, of what still appears by the moonlight, can
be as it was then, when the Big Dipper
noisily collected us. None that it loves
will it ever, as it did us once, carry delightedly.[141]

This poem refers to an actual incident. One bright summer night Paul had an experience, as he described to Ruth, that can be seen as a symbolic expression of his love for her. As they were stargazing together he felt lifted up to the stars with her. For Paul, love was something residing high among the stars, far removed from the earthly. The sexual, however, was suppressed by the twenty-year-old as "will-o'-the-wisps" of his "marshes."[142]

He knows well "what the night wants," and he asks himself: "will my mouth miss the drink of the last wine?" But "the sprites . . . struggled a long time on the heartwall" until "the hour" counted "rosaries instead of flames." Of the beloved, who throws "into the silence, into the distance...slats of flames," he asks that she "bring him quiet sleep." Love is for Paul "a barge... / so heavy with gold and profits that no one rows it." He, nonetheless, "seeks the tiller with a gentle grip," not unlike his "Sindbad" in the poem of the same name.[143]

The sunny summer days of 1940 lasted well into September. Ruth noticed in Paul an approaching melancholy. He no longer wanted to see his old friends, but only to be alone with her. She hoped to cheer him up with a return to their former conviviality. She proposed they take advantage of the beautiful days by joining a group of their friends who were going swimming in the Prut. For Ruth's sake Paul finally consented, but then seemed afraid of showing himself in front of his friends clad only in bathing trunks. Though an excellent swimmer, he only wanted to doze on the bank of the river. It was only Ruth's forceful request that convinced him to go into the water. In the evening, as the cheerful crowd decided to go and called a cab to drive them to the city, Paul began to thaw. His mood changed, and he joined the others singing popular Yiddish and Russian songs.

Usually the drive in the horse-carriage went as far as the Volksgarten Avenue, but because the casino there had been shut down by the Russians, they had to turn around and drive back into the city. They then sat in a run-down café, now called, as all other cafés, a "Restaurant." Despite the proletarian surroundings, the young people entertained themselves regally late into the night.

In lively circles Paul could play the joker. It was as if he sometimes transformed himself into a creature similar to "Puck" in Shakespeare's "Midsummer Night's Dream," who did not so much want to entertain this audience as to make fun of it.[144] In doing this he always quickly became the central figure in the circle of friends, and this seemed perfectly natural to him and his audience. He told amusing stories, imitated well-known personalities, performed scenes from Shakespeare's comedies, or delivered his best version of French or Spanish songs. Paul did not possess a particularly rich voice, but he sang with feeling and confident intonation. And, as a dazzling entertainer, he was confident of the audience's applause.

Even in serious conversation Paul prevailed unchallenged in his circle of friends. His wide reading, his encyclopedic knowledge, his original ideas, and flares of wit made him the center of every discussion. But if someone presented platitudes or nonsense, this could put an abrupt end to Paul's brilliance and cause him to retreat from the circle. In Paul's egocentric behavior one can perhaps recognize, in Hegel's words, the "self-centered-existence" of the creative man, whose imagination sought expression at the same time.

Social relations, however, concealed a danger that Paul, but perhaps not Ruth, had probably foreseen. He wanted to keep his beloved woman for himself and began to watch her suspiciously. A glance or a smile of Ruth's that was not directed at him unsettled him. Since he had confided his true feelings for her to none of his friends, his relationship with her was generally considered to be one of Paul's usual flirtations, and the young men treated Ruth with the usual unrestrained informality.

But Paul suffered from jealousy in silence. He entrusted his suffering only to his poems. However, even though he wrote, he found no release from his jealousy but embroiled himself in it more and more. The feeling was constantly being nurtured anew, and Paul was inexhaustible in the poetic shaping of his anguish.

He writes in the poem "Finsternis" (Darkness), for example: "In your eyes falls betrayal." In "Erinnerung" (Remembrance) the poetic "I" asks:

Und wie war ihr Herz? Ich wusste es nie.
Bis einmal bei Nacht ein Fremder drin schrie.
Den löscht sie mit Tränen aus.

And how was her heart? I never knew.
Until once at night a stranger screamed inside.
She extinguishes him with tears.

His misery is stated more painfully and clearly in the poem "Beieinander" (Together): "At all hours you play with the bright / daggers, but day does not come." In the untitled poem, "I know from the rock into which I dare not go," the middle stanza reads:

Ich weiss von Sternen denen ich nicht glaubte:
es ist ein Weg, ein Weg an Herbstzeitlosen hin . . .
Den führt dich einer mit erhobnem Haupte.
Und du vergisst, wie nah ich bin.

I know from stars that I did not trust:
there is a path, a path along the autumn crocuses . . .
There you are led by one with a raised head.
And you forget how close I am.

Finally, the last stanza contains the desperate prophecy: "a storm is still to come and close all hearts."[145]

Ruth received these poems of jealousy, but her declarations that the poetically expressed suspicions were unfounded were of little help. Paul continued to express his anguish in poetry, even if in a more serene tone:

The Glow of Berenice's Hair

•

Wenn jener kommt in Veilchenkleide,
steckst du ihm an die Finger Ringe,
schlägst um ihn deiner Arme Seide—

Ich sehe und singe.

When he comes robed in violets,
you slide rings onto his fingers,
throw the silk of your arms around him—

I see and sing.

Or in another poem:

Ich lass dich, sieh, an silbernen Gemütern
versuchen was an mir dir nicht gelang...

I let you, look, test on silver souls
what you didn't succeed in doing with me...[146]

There was no evidence in his real life of the willingness to
renounce, alluded to in the poem. Rather, the desperation led
him to ill-considered and apparently not very serious attempts
at suicide. But Paul did not want to die alone. Ruth was to
seek death with him, as a quote from the poem "Schlaflosigkeit"
(Sleeplessness) seems to support:

Ich weiss die Sprüche und du weisst die Gifte.
Der Kelch für beide grünt in meinen Fingern.

Paul Celan

I know the sayings and you know the poisons.
The chalice for both greens in my fingers. [147]

Ruth's explanations that death was pointless and that her own will to live was strong and centered solely on Paul remained unsuccessful. One morning Paul appeared at her home with a bleeding left wrist: "I wanted to die last night," he said tonelessly.

The wound on his wrist was not deep and soon healed. Within himself, however, Paul carried a larger wound that was not to heal so soon: the wound of failure. The young poet had failed because he could not understand love as a reality and not as a dream state, because he could only approach the woman he loved as a sister. "She is my sister, she is my beloved," he writes in the poem "Legend." [148] But the deeper reason for this incapacity is probably grounded in the fact that Paul had also failed to detach himself from his mother, so that anything feminine generally remained taboo to him.

Paul did in fact begin to think about leaving his beloved friend, as the poems clearly show. He writes in "Dornenkranz" (Wreath of Thorns), "The snowlight went out. Alone are all those exposed . . . / I rode into the night; I won't turn back." And the poem "Taglied" (Day Song) also seems to prove a certain determination: "A glimmer remains of what was a life to me . . . Why do you cry, if I now hoist a sail, that slowly darkens as day breaks?" [149] But again he did not act and was not able to detach himself. Nonetheless, it seemed that a certain peacefulness set in for a time.

In the meantime, the winter of 1940–1941 was fierce and stormy. The snow piled up in the streets so that even women were called upon to shovel snow.

In the evenings when walks were not possible, the young people either sat with their books and notepads, or met together

no village nearby, the Romanians had given this name to the camp, which was set in an abandoned quarry and had been used by the Soviets as a disciplinary camp.

While the deportees of 1941 had been spread out over the expansive region of Transnistria, from Schmerinka in the North to near Odessa in the South and closer to the Dniester than to the Bug, and confined there in larger and smaller ghettos, the Romanian rulers sent the deportees of 1942 mainly to the Bug region. There was a very simple reason for this. The Germans on the other bank of the Bug needed laborers because most of the Russian Jews, who had previously provided slave labor, had been liquidated. On the western, Romanian bank, the deported Jews were taken from Cariera de Piatră, divided among several camps, and assigned to road work on the "Thoroughfare #4," which led from Kamenetz to Uman. The overseer of these projects was the "Todt Organization," on close terms with the SS. All Jews unfit for work were transferred to the SS for liquidation.

The abandoned quarry, set on the rocky western bank of the Bug and surrounded by miles of wasteland, appeared to have been specifically created for a camp. Three wooden Soviet barracks remained, as well as the camp commander's villa. Otherwise there were only the remains of destroyed railroad tracks. For three nights the Jews had to remain in the quarry under the open sky in "quarantine," as the presiding officer remarked cynically, before they were let into the barracks. These were filthy and each one could have housed eighteen people. The officers, however, packed 1800 people into the three barracks! Since, nonetheless, all the deportees could not be housed here, many, including Paul's parents, were driven to another camp, eight kilometers away, in the village of Lade-žin. Had Leo and Fritzi Antschel heard, during the three nights spent in the open, the howls of the officers carousing in the commander's villa? Had they heard the screams of the Jewish girls being raped and the fiddling of a Jewish musician, who hadn't been able to part with his violin and now had to play for them?[165]

The Ladežin camp was housed in the ruins of a village school. Surrounded with barbed wire and guarded by Romanian police and Ukrainian auxiliary police, it resembled a small fortress. In the morning after the deportees' arrival, they bartered with villagers on the other side of the fence, who exchanged bread and potatoes for worn-out pieces of clothing. The guards of course also received their share for looking the other way. Those who had nothing to exchange had to go hungry. The soup, served once daily, contained nothing but chick peas generally used only for cattle feed and water. This, as sole nourishment, led to muscle cramps, paralysis of the limbs, bladder trouble, and severe rashes.[166]

Each morning at 4:30, heavy trucks arrived at the camps. The guard teams drove the Jews out of the barracks and loaded them up. The ensuing drive ended at the river, as all the bridges were destroyed, and the Bug was crossed on a ferry. If not everyone found room on it, the transport leader ordered the men to swim across. Those who did not succeed were drowned.

Men and women were forced to work equally. A report about the deportees adds:

> The men lugged stones that the women then smashed into fine gravel with heavy hammers. In the winter they worked on maintaining the roads and clearing the snow. Most of them then had frozen hands, feet, noses, ears. Those who no longer had shoes were considered unfit for

work and were immediately shot. The people of the Todt
Organization kept . . . lists and reported all those unwilling
or unfit for work. These reports were given to the camp
commander, who passed them on to the SS man, who
then had recourse to the SS team brought in especially
for this purpose . . . to murder the victims. Their corpses
were thrown on a pile somewhere, gnawed on by dogs
and pigs and then dragged off. . . . Their relatives never
found out where the murdered victims had been taken. [167]

On August 18, 1942, the Antschels were shipped to the
village of Michailovka. Again they crossed the Bug, then passed
the city of Gaisin. In Michailovka the slaves rented to the Todt
Organization were housed in stables, and only a wooden fence
separated them from the horses, who were better cared for. In
the small room, lit up at night by a tiny petroleum flame—a
wick made of sewing thread burning in a used perfume bottle
containing kerosene—men, women and children lay close to
each other on the bare, hard ground. Some men later had the
courage to settle in the attic of the thatch-roofed stables, until
in the winter the roof collapsed on them under the weight of
the snow. Only the horses were saved, not the people. From
these stables surrounded by barbed wire, men and women were
brought for road work every day before the sun rose.

On October 17, 1942, as Arnold Daghani reported in his
notebook from the time of the deportation, "highly trained
craftsmen were brought to Gaisin. Among them the master
builder Anschel [sic]. Their wives remained in the meantime
in Michailovka." Three days later, Daghani, who had also
stayed behind in Michailovka, noted that several men, and
among them 'Anschel,' "had returned from Gaisin to get their
things. They were uncommunicative about life in Gaisin." [168]

Paul Celan

Paul's 52-year-old father had become more and more emaciated since the Russian invasion. His horrible experiences had turned his hair completely gray and him into a feeble old man hard of hearing. He, like many who no longer possessed any strength at the onset of the cold weather, was simply taken away and shot.

Through the only letter Paul received from his deported mother, he learned of his father's death in the autumn of 1942. Paul never mentioned how this letter reached him from the death-camp. A chaplain may have helped convey it. In the poem "Schwarze Flocken" (Black Flakes) Celan recalls his mother's letter:

Schnee ist gefallen, lichtlos. Ein Mond
ist es schon oder zwei, das der Herbst unter mönchischer Kutte
Botschaft brachte auch mir, ein Blatt aus ukrainischen Halden:
"Denk, das es wintert auch hier, . . .
. . . Kind, ach ein Tuch,
mich zu hüllen darein, wenn es blinket von Helmen,
wenn die Scholle, die rosige, birst, wenn schneeig stäubt das
  Gebein
deines Vaters, unter den Hufen zerknirscht
das Lied von der Zeder. . ."

Snow has fallen, lightless. It is already
one moon or two since the autumn in monkish garb
brought a message also to me, a leaf from Ukrainian hills:

"Think, winter is coming here too, . . .
. . . child, oh for a cloth,
to wrap myself in, when the helmets gleam,
when the floe, the rosy one, bursts, when snow dusts the skeleton

154

of your father, and the Song
of the Cedar is crushed under hoofs. . ."[169]

Paul could not help his mother, who was assigned to the officers' canteen as a cook, much less send her a scarf. He spent the week of mourning, the "shivah," in his grandfather Schrager's home. An understanding Romanian officer had given Paul permission for a short special leave. But no one was allowed to visit him during those seven days. When they had passed, he rushed to the train station, pale, and unshaven.

Paul had never come to terms with his father. The poem "Black Flakes," presumably written toward the end of 1942, is the only poem that refers to his father specifically—and even here the opposition between father and son is revealed in the image, "the Song of the Cedar / is crushed under hoofs." It recalls Leo Antschel's Zionist stance, which Paul did not want to adopt. The "Song of the Cedar" had been sung by Zionists since the times of Theodor Herzl, and it goes in part, "There, where the slender cedar kisses the cloud . . . there, on the shore of the blue sea, my homeland lies."

Celan refers to his father in only one other poem. The volume *Von Schwelle zu Schwelle* contains, along with the "Epitaph for François," Celan's own first son who died in childhood, a poem in memory of his mother, "In Front of a Candle." It also contains "Andenken" (In Memory), in which he speaks of his father in veiled terms:

Feigengenährt sei das Herz,
darin sich die Stunde besinnt
auf das Mandelauge des Toten.
Feigengenährt.
•

Paul Celan

Let the heart be fed with figs,
in which the hour recalls
the dead man's almond eye.
Fed with figs.

The "almond eye" refers, as elsewhere in Celan's work, to
Jews; "fed with figs," to his father's longing for Zion. The
"wrecked forehead" in the second stanza

Schroff, im Anhauch des Meers,
die gescheiterte
Stirne,
die Klippenschwester.

Jagged, in the ocean's breath,
the wrecked
forehead,
the sister of cliffs.

conceals his father's failure to achieve his Zionist dream. But
in referring to the forehead as "the sister of cliffs," the poem
indicates that his father, stranded on the cliff, will never reach
the "shore of the blue sea" as in the Zionist song. Finally, the
"white hair" mentioned in the third and last stanza

Und um dein Weisshaar vermehrt
das Vlies
der sömmernden Wolke.

And your white hair adds to
the fleece
of the summering cloud.

•

refers to Paul's last meeting with his father under the "summering cloud" of June 1942.[170]

"With a Variable Key," the title and first line of another poem from *Von Schwelle zu Schwelle,* Celan seeks the repressed, ambivalent emotions within himself and tries to open "the house in which / drifts the snow of that left unsaid." But because this "snow of that left unsaid," the unconscious, "will cluster round the word," as the last line of this poem says, the poetic resolution of this conflict does not succeed.[171]

And so it was not so much the hard physical labor, hunger, and cold, that led Paul to become more and more melancholic, as it was the tremendous guilt that he survived while his parents suffered a gruesome death. As early as the beginning of 1943, he wrote: "What would it be, mother: growth or wound—/ if I were also to drown in the snow drifts of the Ukraine?"[172] When, in the course of this winter, he learned from an escaped relative[173] that his mother had been shot in the back of the neck, he wrote: "Oh stone masts of melancholy! Oh I among you and alive! / Oh I among you and alive and beautiful, and she's not allowed to smile to me..."[174]

In the darkness of wartime and the mourning for his dead parents, Paul's life had also grown dark. The "dream of a dream"—the expression Celan borrowed from Rilke to characterize his life before the outbreak of the war—had become as black as the rose in the poem "Ein Rosenkelch" (A Rose Goblet):

Rosen im einsamen Helm: . . .
Tau fiel nur spärlich und rings, schwer und mit fremder Gebärde,
heben sich . . . die Schwingen der furchtbaren Engel,
Gram zu verteilen euch allen. Den gelben, den weissen, den
    roten . . .

Paul Celan

Eben glitt Laub in ein Grab, das keine der Schwestern euch
schmückt,
... Erst wenn die schwarze nicht fehlt, die mein Herz mir
gezogen,
blendet kein Strahl mir das Aug und kein Feuer versengt mir
die Braue,
trifft mich kein Pfeil und keiner mehr spannt hier den
Bogen. . . .

Roses in the lonely helmet: . . .
Dew fell only sparsely and all around, heavy with foreign
gestures,
the wings of the dreadful angels . . . rise up, . . .
to distribute grief to you all. To the yellow, the white, the red
ones . . .
Leaves just now slipped into a grave, which none of the sisters
adorns for you,
. . . Only when the black one is not absent, that pulled my
heart from me,
will no beam blind my eyes and no fire singe my brows,
no arrow strike me and none here continue to draw the bow
taut . . . [175]

Only now, after the death of his parents, did the Jewish
element find its way into Paul's writing. He identified their
fate with his people's suffering over thousands of years:

Nur die Nacht vor den Augen lass reden:
. . . Nur sie, nur sie allein.
Dich aber tritt mit dem Fuss und sprich zu dir selber: Sei tapfer,
sei würdig des Steins über dir,

Towards the Abyss

bleib Freund mit den Bärten der Toten,
füg Blume zu Wurm,
hiss dein Segel auf Särgen,
... hiss dein Segel auf Särgen,
bette dein Herz dir zu Häupten.

Allow only the night to speak before your eyes:
... Only she, the night alone.
But you, kick yourself and say to yourself: be courageous,
be worthy of the stone above you,
remain friendly with the beards of the dead,
push flower to worm,
hoist your sail on coffins,
... hoist your sail on coffins,
bed your heart by your head.[176]

In this miserable spring of 1943, Paul was consoled only
by his poetry and thoughts of Ruth, with whom he was able
to correspond. On March 19, 1943, he wrote to her of himself
as if of someone else:

> He is happy to know that, in his poems, the wonderful
> often gained permanence, that, stirring at the heart's fron-
> tier, something intimate was meant to describe what was
> unspeakably great.

And on March 28:

> They say spring is now coming... For about two years
> now I no longer feel the seasons and flowers, and nights
> and transformations at all—as many [poems] as were dear

to me, I know are through me in your possession, and whatever is to become of me that cannot bloom before you has to fade away.

On April 6 he wrote very matter-of-factly:

A request, concerning my poems: do not bind the translations with the rest of the poems (rather not at all); do not write a name on the title page and no title, at most "Poems."

In an undated letter from the same period, he wrote:

In any case I believe that your book—if it ever becomes a book—is self-contained, at most I would be able to add a few poems.

Paul already considered the poems, the "book," a bequest to Ruth. He seems to regard not only his poetry, but also his life as concluded or "self-contained." What he no longer hopes for himself, however, is to be granted to his poetry: a continuation of life in the future, but without his name, which has become meaningless to him. His work is to bear witness to that "unspeakably great" thing which had moved him.

In the summer of 1943—even under a burning sun, the slave labor with the shovel continued uninterrupted—Paul's longing for Ruth and the gardens, the witnesses of their love, was particularly intense. On August 23 he wrote to her:

I want to place something in your hands, . . . as in the past my life was placed in your hands, strange, in the whirl and noise. What I can give you across the distance,

Towards the Abyss

as a glimmer, as a gentle call (where is the elegance of
the star-bright heart, where is the euphoria of gardens?)
is only a poem. It wants, for a moment (or for many?) to
let the breath of a southern landscape blow through your
hair, and when the sea then again releases your gaze, one
who tarries in the dark, nearby, hopes to remain with the
waves of the only reality. The poem follows a Provençal
song that you perhaps know: "O Magali, ma tant amato,
mete ta teste au fenestroun" (O Magali, ma tant aimée,
mets ta tête au fenêtron).

To his poem he gives the title "Das Fenster im Südturm"
(Window in the South Tower):

Pfeile gehn in schrägen
tiefgrünen Sträussen niedcr in den Rosenhag—
. . .
wo der Jasmin den Blick allein lässt, ist das Meer—
und weiter unten ist dic Welt zuende.
. . .
Hier wird dein Herz, dem schwarzen Stern entrissen,
mir leicht sein wie cin Mondstrahl, Magali.

Arrows blow in oblique
deep-green bunches into the rose-grove—
. . .
where the jasmine leaves its gaze is the sea—
and further down the world comes to an end.
. . .
Here, your heart, torn from the black star,
will be as light to me as a moonbeam, Magali.[177]

•

Paul Celan

The end of the summer put an end to the dream of a southern world. And autumn brought a poem named after this time of year:

Verteilt ist der sündige Efeu. Die Fahnen niedergeholt.
Erklungen sind Sense und Speer: die Leier vielleicht.

The sinful ivy has been doled out. The flags pulled down.
Scythe and spear rang out: the lyre perhaps. [178]

In the beginning of 1944 there was talk of secret negotiations for a separate peace between Romania and the Soviet Union. Rumors surfaced that the Jews—and first among them the numerous orphaned children—would be allowed to return home from Transnistria. But nothing happened. Suddenly in February, however, the Jews in forced labor were quietly granted time off, without a date for their return. As later became clear, this was the final, but not officially admitted, dissolution of the camps.

Paul was back in the city. The situation of the Jews, however, remained uncertain. Although Hitler's armies were in retreat, the SS rearguards continued the liquidation of the Jews in many places, so that the hope of surviving only slowly became greater than the continued fear of falling into the hands of the SS.

The Romanian authorities, meanwhile, became more lenient toward the Jews and allowed them a certain freedom of movement, so that even larger groups could convene in private homes, which had previously been strictly prohibited. The young people took advantage of this and gathered at friends' homes, discussed the situation, and made plans for the future. The tendency of all social circles to fraternize was new. The persecution they suffered had united the Jews, and those who had been separated by their opinions or by social barriers before the war now socialized.

So Paul met, for the first time, a girl from a formerly wealthy middle-class home, who had admired him from a distance in the Gymnasium and often heard him mentioned as a budding poet. In a conversation in 1972, she reminisced about this encounter:

> It was a cold winter evening, and Paul stood by the tall tiled stove and glanced about absently. A smile that was tinged with something like contempt for everything around him was frozen on his face. He was good-looking, the way he stood there, upright and with this contempt in his eyes. He seemed like a distant, unapproachable idol. Paul was silent throughout the entire evening. I did not make his acquaintance then, that came much later, but this first impression remained forever.[179]

Paul spent his days mainly with Ruth and her parents and sometimes visited old friends with her. He was in his room—he lived again with grandfather Schrager—almost only at night. The old, half-crumbled home, in which the aged Philipp Schrager lived by himself since the death of his wife, did not attract Paul in the least, although his grandfather was a kind and pleasant man. "I can't bear the smell of poverty there," Paul is reported to have said, "no nature nearby, not even a tree can be seen there."[180]

During this time Paul also made the acquaintance, through Chaim Ginniger, of Rose Ausländer, who says the following of him:

●

Paul Celan

After Paul's first visit to my place, which he had made with Ginniger, he visited me a few more times. He read from his poetry and I was very enthusiastic about Paul's poems from the beginning. Although his style did not at all correspond to mine, I approved of it and encouraged Paul to continue his poetic work.

That Paul used the metaphor "black milk"—which I had employed in the poem "Ins Leben" [Into Life] written in 1925, but not published until 1939—for his "Death Fugue" seems only natural to me, because a poet is allowed to use everything as material for his own poetry. It honors me that a great poet found a stimulus in my early work. I had not used the metaphor at all negligently, but he has raised it to the highest level of poetic expression. It has become a part of him.

I did not see Paul again until 1946 by chance in Bucharest, but there was no possibility for an actual discussion, as I was completely occupied with my preparations to emigrate.[181]

Paul also resumed friendly relations with Edith. When in the house of her father, the Germanist Horowitz, the conversation by chance touched on the "Nibelungenlied," and Paul confessed his ignorance in this area, Dr. Horowitz offered to introduce him to Middle High German literature.[182] Glad to be able to overcome the stagnation in his accumulation of knowledge that had set in during the war, Paul was an enthusiastic student—and this knowledge entered his poetry. Poems like "Die letzte Fahne" (The Last Flag) and "Ein Lied in der Wüste" (A Song in the Desert) take up images of knighthood. They were written after 1944 and later collected in the volume *Der Sand aus den Urnen*. In language inspired by medieval German heroic poetry, Paul seemed to find a suitable medium with which he could poetically confront the crime perpetrated by his German contemporaries.[183]

With the signs of a late spring in 1944, the Romanian police suddenly resumed a strict surveillance of the Jews—the German command, which had to ensure its retreat, had again imposed a tighter grip on Romania. Paul braved the renewed curfew and went to the Volksgarten, prohibited to Jews, in order to observe the awakening of nature as in the past. He was promptly arrested by a police patrol and taken to jail, but was let off with a beating. To his friends' questions about the reason for his bruised face, he simply replied: "I wanted to see the Volksgarten again!"[184]

At the beginning of April Czernowitz was bombed several times by the Soviets, who were already on the Dniester. In the same month, the Red Army moved into the city unopposed.

X

Alien Homeland

Setz dein Fahne auf Halbmast,	Set your flag at half-mast,
Errinnrung.	memory.
Auf Halbmast	At half-mast
für heute und immer.	today and for ever.

Herz:	Heart:
Gib dich auch hier zu erkennen,	Here too reveal what you are,
hier, in der Mitte des Marktes.	here, in the midst of the market.
Ruf's, das Shibboleth, hinaus	Call the Shibboleth, call it out
in die Fremde der Heimat:	into your alien homeland:
Februar: no pasaran.	February: *no pasarán.*

T HE Red Army soldiers were no longer smiling during this second occupation of Czernowitz, and the Soviet commanders, without exception, treated the civilian population with the harshness of conquerors. In their eyes, the inhabitants of the Bukovina had collaborated with German and Romanian troops, and as far as they were concerned, everyone was guilty, including the Jews. The accounts of their suffering under Nazi rule did not impress Soviet soldiers. "Russischer Frühling" (Russian Spring) was Paul's name for this peculiar time in the title of a poem which contains the following lines:

Gestürzt ist der Helm voller Blut: . . .

. . .

Knie, es wird Zeit nun zu knien, in den Orgelstimmen von einst

Paul Celan

dröhnt es nun laut und ich muss mit Jakobs Engel noch ringen?
Allein mit den jüdischen Gräbern, weiss ich, Geliebte, du
weinst...

The helmet full of blood is upturned:...
...
Kneel, it is time now to kneel, the organ voices of yesterday
now rumble loudly and must I still wrestle with Jacob's angel?
Alone with the Jewish graves, I know, beloved, you weep...[185]

Once again, the Russians needed "volunteers" and unpaid
laborers to dismantle bombed-out buildings, destroy Romanian
civilian archives, and collect books from abandoned homes.
But the equal treatment of the different ethnic groups could
not reconcile the Jews with the fact that they again had to
provide forced labor.

Paul had to collect books. One could see him in the
Herrengasse, a heavy stack of books in his arms, bent over a
handcart loaded with more books. Once, when Paul stood up
straight, he saw before him a Soviet officer in jackboots—a
revolver in his belt—scrutinizing him in a peculiar way. Paul
recognized him as an old acquaintance from the anti-fascist
circle. The former companion's martial disguise did not prevent
Paul from flinging his arms around his neck and exclaiming:
"You're back again!"[186]

In addition to forced labor, a new danger threatened the
Jews from a different flank. Since the war was still continuing
and the Russians needed auxiliary troops, they began to draft
Jewish recruits because Jews still seemed to make the most
reliable soldiers. The recruited Jews were mostly assigned to
the Polish Legion in neighboring Galicia. But as this legion

was considered particularly anti-Semitic, many Jews sought to escape and some of them, who had once studied in Prague or Brno and were well-versed in Czech, succeeded in being accepted by the Czechoslovak Legion stationed in Sadagora near Czernowitz.[187]

Since Paul was also subject to military service but under no circumstances wanted to be sent to the anti-Semitic legion, he also sought a way out. His friends Jakob Silbermann and Hersh Segal offered advice. Segal's brother-in-law, the psychiatrist Dr. Pinkas Mayer, director of the state asylum, was in need of assistant medical personnel. And so Paul, the former medical student, was employed in the psychiatric clinic as "assistant to the doctor" (in Russian "lekarstvi pomocz" or "lekpom" for short), and was thus exempted from military service.[188]

During his first encounter with the mentally ill, Paul tried to immerse himself in their world and in so doing to apply his knowledge of psychoanalysis. At the time, he only knew the basic outlines of Freud's teaching, although he had attempted earlier to analyse his own verbal slips in the spirit of Freud. When Paul was approached, during his work at the clinic, with an offer to accompany a transport of patients to Kiev, he firmly declined. He was completely uninterested in a trip into the interior regions of the Soviet Union, as all of his hopes were directed to possible paths to the West.[189]

The Russians needed single women as workers for the coal mines in the Donets Basin. Ruth Lackner describes their difficult situation:

It was an ugly time: girls and women were stopped in broad daylight by militia soldiers. Those who could not prove that they were married or employed were stamped "persons of easy-going morals" requiring "re education"

Paul Celan

in a labor camp. After a few weeks, the radio announced that several thousand "prostitutes" had "voluntarily" registered for resettlement in the Union's interior to become productive people. If not enough women were to be found in the streets, they came looking for them in their homes. It was not until the autumn of 1944 that the arrests stopped.

In the meantime, survivors began to return from Transnistria. Among them were Paul's aunt, Regina Rones, her husband, and their daughter. When asked about the fate of Leo and Fritzi Antschel, they could not report more than what Paul already knew. They had encountered them once during the transfer from one camp to another, but only for a few moments. They were immediately separated and loaded into heavy trucks with different destinations.

After their return, Paul succeeded in regaining control of his parents' home, to which he now had rights, as he was to live there together with his relatives. And as a result, his aunt Regina cared for her orphaned nephew like a mother.

Two Bukovinian poets also returned from exile, Alfred Kittner and Immanuel Weissglas, whom Paul met at Rose Ausländer's.[190] In silence he followed their reports about life in the camp with its horrors and inhuman conditions. That Weissglas had succeeded in rescuing his old mother deepened Paul's feelings of guilt. From the harshest time of his life, Paul's former schoolmate brought poems which sought to come to terms with the suffering. As in the Gymnasium years, Weissglas made an effort to establish a "poetic friendship" with Paul, but his poems did not correspond to Paul's feelings and linguistic eloquence. "There was nothing in common between Paul Antschel and Immanuel Weissglas," attests Rose Ausländer.

Alien Homeland

"Each of them read me his own poems. I never heard of any kind of collaboration."

Alfred Kittner, whom Paul, 14 years younger, did not get to know until after his return from exile, already had behind him a certain career as a German-language journalist and poet. But Kittner, who wrote very conventional poems, "resolutely rejected Paul's much too personal metaphors," as Rose Ausländer reports.[191] Paul was and remained a loner of a highly individual character.

In the autumn of 1944 the Soviets once again reopened the Russian-Ukrainian university, and Paul was able to resume his studies. This time he signed up for English studies—he wanted to perfect his knowledge of English and especially of Shakespeare's language. And perhaps he did this with the intention of more extensive translations of the poet; in his little black notebook of that time, which he had carried with him in the camp, there already appears a translation of Shakespeare's Sonnet 57. Whenever he was dissatisfied with the professors' lectures, Paul went ahead on his own, and the university library, which had fortunately not been plundered, was a great help to him in his work.

Even in this new era of the Soviet Czernowitz university, the students were given a salary. But since the sum no longer sufficed for the much more difficult circumstances of the year 1944, Paul had to seek out additional sources of income. So he translated contemporary articles and texts of "progressive" authors of Romanian literature for the local Ukrainian newspaper.

At this time another circle, composed for the most part of girls, formed around Paul. In his friendly relations with female university colleagues, with whom he did not have to fear any emotional complications, he found a certain relief

Paul Celan

from his increasingly difficult relationship with Ruth. He even spoke, for the first time, to others of his feelings for her. Dorothea became his "father confessor,"[192] and she reports on the time after the resumption of university studies:

> When he decided, in 1944, to study English literature, he enchanted us with declamations of his beloved Shakespearean sonnets, or the darkly overcast verses of Blake. This genius of language was also a language-genius. . . . He, who had to earn his meagre bread as translator for a pitiful local paper, now only bore an exterior resemblance to the student of the 1940s. The once so beautiful home of his parents had been robbed of its greatest valuables and there was not even a tombstone to warm with hot tears and trembling hands.[193]

Paul had without a doubt undergone a transformation: suffering had left behind indelible traces. The cheerfulness, which one could often perceive in him earlier, had been left in the same past as the play-acting and similar amusements. The changes in his exterior were also noticeable. The once meticulously-dressed Paul, who would not tolerate a speck of dust on his clothes, now valued his appearance considerably less. But this was surely also a result of the current circumstances. "The beautiful vests that his mother had once knitted had become flimsy and threadbare," and at the university, "body and soul would freeze in the unheated lecture halls," as Dorothea Müller-Altneu reports.[194]

The mental changes, however, were especially noticeable in encounters with old friends, who had been reduced to a small circle. Unexpectedly, Paul would recite Yiddish fables from Steinbarg or suddenly sing quietly to himself a ritual melody from the New Year's service. For the first time they heard Paul speak of the beauty of the Hebrew language and talk of the years he had spent learning Hebrew.[195] And during this time Paul also began to read Martin Buber's writings intensively: the "Three Lectures on Judaism" and "The Hasidic Tales."[196]

Eastern Europe had now been freed from German soldiers, but the war continued and intensified the longing for peace in all the affected regions. In this corner of Europe, however, which had once been called Czernowitz—the Russians wrote "Chernovtsy"—the longing for an end to the war concealed a particular desire: to be able to leave the fatherland, which was becoming more and more alien. After the experiences of 1940 and the ensuing years of the war, very few Jews wanted to remain Soviet citizens. But the path to the West was closed.

In the poems created during this time, traces of this hope and doubt concerning the end of the war can be recognized. In "Flügelrauschen" (Swishing of Wings), for instance:

. . .
Die Taube aber säumt in Avalun.

Der Ölzweig ward geraubt von Adlerschnäbeln
und wo dein Lager blaut im schwarzen Zelt zerpflückt.
. . .
[Ich] rief. . .
den Vogel an, ein Werk des Trosts zu tun.
Er malt dir in das Aug die Schattenkrallen.

Ich aber seh die Taube kommen, weiss, aus Avalun.

•

175

Paul Celan

. . .
Yet the dove tarries in Avalon.

The olive-branch was robbed by eagles' beaks
and picked to pieces in the black tent where your camp dawns.
. . .
[I] called . . .
on the bird to perform an act of consolation
He paints into your eyes his shadow-claws.

Yet I see the dove coming, white, from Avalon.

Or, with less confidence in the approaching relief from all the
horrors of wartime, in "Der Pfeil der Artemis" (Artemis' Arrow):

Die Zeit tritt ehern in ihr letztes Alter.
Nur du allein bist silbern hier.
. . .
Wie soll, der über himmelblauen Kies
sich mit den Nymphen drehte, leicht,
nicht denken, dass ein Pfeil der Artemis
im Wald noch irrt und ihn zuletzt erreicht?

Time brazenly enters its last age.
You alone are silver here.
. . .
How is he who spun round with the
nymphs above sky-blue pebbles, lightly,
not to think that Artemis' arrow
still strays in the woods and in the end may strike him?[197]

In these uncertain times one thing seemed, nonetheless,

to have become a certainty for Paul: poetry was his vocation and destiny. What he had regarded in his letters from the labor camp as a farewell and a bequest became a new beginning. Shortly after his return to the city, Paul had assembled, with the help of his friends Segal and Silbermann, a first collection of his poems and duplicated it on a typewriter. This "Typescript 1944" bears the title "Poems" and no author's name—Paul thus realized what he had imagined as the future exterior appearance of his "book," described in the letter written to Ruth from the labor camp on April 6, 1943.[198] Many of the poems written on loose sheets of paper before 1944 were not included in the collection—poems whose themes suggest they were created during the time of persecution by Romanian Fascists and German Nazis. On the other hand, older poems are included that do not appear in any later collection. One can assume, therefore, that Paul considered this first selection, encompassing 93 poems, the bulk of his early poems that were worthy of survival.[199]

In the autumn of 1944 Paul began to prepare a second, this time handwritten, collection of his poems and he finished the project early in 1945. The manuscript was to be a present for Ruth, but it brought out a desire in Paul to submit it for assessment to a well-known poet from the Bukovina, Alfred Margul-Sperber, who lived in Bucharest.

Paul's plan, to take a step toward greater publicity for his poems at this precise moment, did not come to him by chance. In Czernowitz rumors were already circulating about Soviet intentions to expel all the Jews from the Bukovina. This expulsion, it was said, was to be disguised as an apparently voluntary emigration to Romania, and soon administrative measures would be taken and applications for emigration would be accepted. The border between the Soviet and the Romanian

Paul Celan

halves of the Bukovina was in fact already being guarded less strictly, and several Jews had already succeeded in crossing secretly. Ruth also wanted to attempt an early border crossing to escape from the unbearable conditions as soon as possible, and she was to establish contact with Margul-Sperber in Bucharest. Paul too was planning his emigration, but, being bound to his aunt and her family, he had to wait for the official emigration permit.

Due to a shortage of good writing paper, Paul used an advertising calendar from before the war for the new collection, which, with its black leather binding, gave the impression of being a real, published book. Paul included 97 poems in this collection, written in calligraphic handwriting, many of them from his richly productive period of 1943–1944. His selection of the poems was undoubtedly more stringent than for the "Typescript 1944." If Margul-Sperber had considered the poems publishable, then the manuscript itself could have been used to print. For the first time in any case, Paul was hoping for the publication of a real book, according to Ruth Lackner.

Margul-Sperber, about whom Paul had heard much talk and some of whose work he might even have read without ever having met him, had been a contributor to the "Czernowitzer Morgenblatt" (Czernowitz Morning Paper) before the war. In this capacity he had sometimes been able to publish the work of young poets. But Paul had never turned to him or to any of the other local dailies and magazines for the publication of a poem. He had been in no rush to see himself published.

He chose Margul-Sperber in particular, probably for the simple reason that this poet's name was well-known. But had Paul been acquainted with Margul-Sperber's poetry, he might have been particularly impressed by the dedication of his first volume of poems, "Gleichnisse der Landschaft" (Landscape Allegories)—"To the Memory of My Mother"—and with an untitled poem that opens the volume and whose last lines are as follows: "Everywhere the mother wakes forever through the / glassy room and sings into dream." The fact that Margul-Sperber wrote in the introduction to his volume of poems that he dedicates himself "openly to everything antiquated and conventional in form, choice and treatment of [his] poetic subjects," may not have exactly encouraged Paul to submit his poems to him. [200]

From the beginning Paul connected his hope of emigration with his intention to reach Vienna. He had always dreamed of the old imperial city as "that which was within reach" but "still to be reached" and truly still believed it would be filled with a mysterious magic. [201] Reality, however, forced him to revise his childhood longing: he had to understand that Vienna, after Nazi rule and under Soviet occupation, could no longer fulfill the hopes he had for it.

So it happened that he explained to Ruth one day, shortly before her emigration: "The main thing is to get away from here. Where one winds up is irrelevant, so long as there's freedom there. How would it be, for instance, to arrive in Jerusalem, to go to Martin Buber, and to say to him, 'Uncle Buber, here I am, here you have me!'" Only the joker in Paul, however, spoke of Palestine, while many Jews now thought in all seriousness about emigrating there. [202]

In the few months between Ruth's departure and Paul's emigration, he was seized by a new passion for a woman. At the university in 1940 he had met Rosa Leibovici, who, because of her communist convictions, had come from Romanian Iaşi to Soviet-occupied Czernowitz. As she initially arrived alone and without means, the students had helped Rosa as much as they could. As a result she had befriended one of her school-mates, Tanya, and now lived with her. Paul apparently belonged to the circle of friends and protectors of the two girls. Now, in Ruth's absence, his initial sympathy with Rosa, who was said to have been as pretty as a picture, turned into love. They were seen together all the time and considered a happy couple, and everyone was glad that Rosa had found a male friend.[203]

In April 1945 Paul and his relatives were finally able to prepare for emigration to Romania. Like all the other emigrants, they were registered, but no one received a passport—this was the Russian method of discreetly deporting unwanted groups of people.

Paul Antschel left his hometown forever. But in his future wanderings, and even in Paris, he was accompanied by the "Meridian" of his place of birth. He remembered this "Meridian" again and again, not only in the Büchner Prize speech of 1960, but also in later letters to his countrymen. In 1962 he wrote to a former university colleague: "Je suis loin, bien sûr, je suis toujours près . . . de mon méridien."[*][204] And even later, in 1968, he was to write a countryman about Gustav Landauer and Leon Kellner "in reference to my (Czernowitz) Meridian,"[205] which connected the fatherland with the "heart-wall."[206]

The trip to Bucharest was arduous. They sat crushed together in a Russian military truck, as the train service, interrupted during the retreat of the Romanians, had not yet been restored. But what did the crush matter when the whole wide world seemed to be awaiting him! Upon his arrival in the Romanian capital, Paul received good news from Ruth. Mar-

---

[*]"I am far away, of course, I am always close . . . to my Meridian." —M.B.

gul-Sperber, who had been fascinated with Paul's poems and was expecting him impatiently, wanted to do what he could to find a publisher for him.

Paul rushed to Sperber's and was hospitably received. As a result he visited him often and always received a warm welcome. But the conversation rarely turned to Paul's poetry—Paul was satisfied with the recognition the older poet had shown toward his poetry, which had given him a confidence he had hitherto lacked. He had never before been interested in discussions of his poems, and so it remained.[207]

Bucharest, which Paul saw as simply a leg on his trip to Vienna, was to keep him for two years, since the Romanian authorities did not issue travel documents to refugees from northern Bukovina. The borders could be crossed only clandestinely, and for this, one needed money and courage. As Paul was lacking both, he was forced to wait.

In this time of great changes the problem of the relationship between Paul and Ruth continued to await a solution. For Paul this attachment to Ruth, who now distanced herself from him more and more, had been an emotional experience whose fulfillment remained a failure. Now, in Bucharest, a serious conflict erupted between them and ended with the final renunciation of any possible life together. Nonetheless, the friendship remained intact, since the emotional bond was so intense that it could not be torn from either one of them. And Ruth still remained the first to read Paul's new poems.

Since Paul was now without means, he had at least to find temporary work and to look for inexpensive living quarters. When he saw his friend Leonid Miller again, he immediately accepted an offer to share student lodgings. He also chanced to meet other friends everywhere he went in Bucharest, and although he was not inclined to renew old relationships with

the former student of Romance languages and literature also remembered a thirteenth-century Italian philosopher, Thomas of Celano, the poet and biographer of Francis of Assisi.

Paul became "very close" friends with the Romanian-Jewish poet Petre Solomon,[213] who wrote exclusively in Romanian, and this friendship was still to prove substantial many years later, during Solomon's visits to Paris. As Solomon knew that Celan was perfectly fluent in Romanian, he tried to incite Paul to write poetry in this language. For the sake of his friend, Paul wrote a few Romanian poems and prose texts, and he made a gift of them to Solomon. These Romanian compositions in bound form are no less accomplished than the German poems in *Mohn und Gedächtnis* and are particularly remarkable for their rich vocabulary.[214]

Still, Paul did not want to become a Romanian poet. He answered everyone who reproached him for writing in the language of his parents' murderers: "Only in one's mother tongue can one express one's own truth, in a foreign language the poet lies."[215] And in 1961 he specified that "Poetry is a fateful and unique instance of language," and added that he did not believe in "bilingualism in poetry."[216]

Paul's Bucharest years, the first of his independent life far from home, transformed his lifestyle. Gradually his talents and character traits began to develop and shed their constrictions. Petre Solomon writes about this:

> I remember him as young and tenacious, as someone who held his head high under the burden of misery and was full of joie de vivre. A joy, that had something artificial about it, as if he, as the Romanian saying goes, wanted to "pound fun out of misfortune." He loved word-play and untiringly dispensed his witticisms, which became so

numerous that I found myself having to record them in an "Evening Booklet of Paul Celan." . . . The two years spent in Bucharest were among the happiest of his storm-tossed life. The secret of this happiness? The friendly relationships he was able to initiate here in a time of dramatic happenings and great difficulties.[217]

Celan found, not least through his work in publishing, rapid access to the literary life in Bucharest, of which Jewish-Romanian literary figures were an important part. Only as an exception did he mix with non-Jewish circles—Petre Solomon, for instance, introduced him to the poet and dramatist Maria Bănuş. That she also translated Rilke into Romanian must have interested Celan in particular. And he met Ion Caraion, one of the most popular and influential Romanian poets of the time, on only one occasion—when he submitted poems to him for the "Agora" magazine. But Celan nurtured friendly relations with Jewish personalities like the young poet Nina Cassian,[218] the critic Ovid Crohmălniceanu and the writers Gellu Naum and Marcel Aderca. His connection to Romanian literary figures led to repeated, but unsuccessful attempts to entice Celan to write in Romanian. So the few poems written for Petre Solomon are the only evidence of Celan's talent in this language.

Although Celan was to leave this circle behind secretly and without farewell, the friendships were still maintained later; Petre Solomon, Ovid Crohmălniceanu, and others visited Celan in Paris or met up with him in Germany. After Celan's death, Crohmălniceanu, for instance, spoke "of him only as Paul" and told about "his pleasant way of joking, the strange swings in his moods, about the . . . atmosphere of their meeting again in Paris."[219]

Paul Celan

Such old friendships, as well as new ones, contributed greatly to the strengthening of Celan's self-confidence. But these emotional and social relationships did not suffice to gain him an internal self-assurance. What he finally needed above all was an assertion, important for himself, of his masculinity.

What Celan had found impossible in his love for Ruth, overshadowed by the bond to his mother, now came easily to him with women, whom he could at last face uninhibitedly. The taboo of the feminine, established in his childhood, began to lose its force, and he no longer struggled against the experience of his own sexuality. From time to time, he would complain to a friend that the easy girls with whom he came into contact were awfully primitive, but this fact did not keep him from their company.[220]

Rosa Leibovici, who had originally not wanted to leave Czernowitz, finally allowed herself to be convinced, solely by Celan's repeated declarations of love, to come to Bucharest. The two were again seen as an inseparable couple, and since Ruth Lackner had married in the meantime, Celan's relationship with Rosa was regarded as a happy and lasting bond.

Celan experienced the highpoint of his social relations in the circle of Bucharest surrealists around Ghérasim Luca,[221] D. Trost and Paul Păun. Whereas Luca, who had founded the circle in 1939 after his return from Paris and maintained contact with André Breton, published theoretical books in French, Păun wrote Romanian verse.[222] Most of the circle's members, however, were painters and sculptors who had adopted the style of the Paris surrealists. In addition there were many art-lovers who were effusive enthusiasts of surrealism. Social gatherings, in which beautiful women also participated, united them all. They met in cafés and restaurants and there payed homage to Bacchus and the "muse" of the circle, the Frenchwoman Nadine. This social activity in particular was an incentive for Paul to join the circle. Here too, where Celan was the only German-language poet, his poetry was never discussed. If he gathered artistic stimulation from the surrealist club, then it was probably only from the exterior activities of the circle—Celan never managed to develop any deep friendships with them.

In 1946 the Bucharest surrealists organized an exhibition with paintings, sculptures, and objects, which caused a sensation and raised much interest. Paul Celan went with Ruth and saw the "Expoziție Surrealistă" with great pleasure, but as an outsider.

Paul's relationship with Rosa Leibovici, which initially seemed to be a very intimate one, suffered a sudden rupture after a few months—probably through a fault of Paul's, whose "loves, flaring up, blazing, and dying out like straw"[223] were remembered years later by his friends. Rosa, whose sincere love for Celan is emphasized in her descriptions of their relationship, was married in the 1950s to a high Romanian government official, but she died of tuberculosis early in the 1960s. Celan, who received the news of her death in Paris, was said to have been deeply distressed.[224] Thus it is not impossible that his poem "Coagula," which begins with the lines, "Your wound / as well, Rosa," refers not only to Rosa Luxemburg,* but also to the personally important Rosa Leibovici, who was from the Moldova valley, home to the "Romanian buffaloes" of which the poem also speaks.[225]

In connection with this, an early friend of Celan's points out that he had always been fascinated by thoughts of his own

*Rosa Luxemburg and Karl Liebknecht were founders of the revolutionary German Communist Worker's Party (KPD) and became the martyred heroes of the 1919 Spartacus revolt in Berlin. —M.B.

Paul Celan

death and that he was, in particular, very strangely moved by the suicides of people he knew, as if those suicides represented an exhortation for himself. In 1940, in Czernowitz, a girl who had been seduced and then abandoned by a Red Army soldier committed suicide. And in 1946 another girl likewise found no solution other than death when she had been abandoned by a Romanian. On each occasion Celan reacted with heartfelt depression to the news of his acquaintances' deaths.[226]

Intensive translation work in the publishing house, readings mainly of Russian poets, enjoyable evenings in the tight circle of friends or with the surrealists, who seemed to be more concerned with the shaping of their lives than with art and literature—all this constituted the "Mohn" (poppy) of forgetfulness in Celan's waiting period in Bucharest. At night, however, in the solitude of his furnished room, now inhabited by him alone, where a sense of belonging and a feeling of being at home could hardly have surfaced, he wrote poems that were dedicated to "Gedächtnis" (memory). The majority of the poems published in his first collected volume *Der Sand aus den Urnen*, of which many were later reprinted in *Mohn und Gedächtnis*, came into being during these Bucharest nights.

Time passed, and the firmer Celan's footing in Bucharest became, the stronger was his desire to continue his migration— to Vienna. As the chances of legal emigration remained slim, he began to consider an illegal border-crossing. Together with three friends from the surrealists' circle (Paul Păun, Ghérasim Luca, and Dolfi Trost) he planned an escape attempt, which, nonetheless, never took place.[227]

Celan tried again to escape in August 1947. In the company of a young Romanian woman, he appeared at the house of his countryman Arnold Daghani, now also living in Bucharest, and proposed that the three of them escape together.

Daghani, however, had to decline because he lacked the necessary money.[228]

In December of 1947 Paul decided to venture the crossing on his own. It was high time for him to leave the country, as political developments in Romania showed a decisive trend toward single-party rule of the Communists. They were in the process of crushing the opposition of the Peasants' Party and of the Liberals, incorporating the Social Democrats into their party, and abolishing the monarchy. The Sovietization of Romania was, after all, a fait accompli.

The people in the publishing house knew nothing of Celan's intentions, but spoke, on the contrary, of the brilliant future that lay ahead of him. That is what he seemed to be alluding to when he said, while taking his leave from his friend Leonid Miller, "I am crown-prince at the publisher's," and added laughingly, "but I'm going up and away!"[229]

Otherwise, he said goodbye to only a few of his trusted friends—to Ruth, to Corina Marcovici, one of Paul's Bucharest girlfriends, and to Margul-Sperber—and left all of them with manuscripts of his poetry. So Ruth kept the little black leather book and a number of loose sheets with poems from different periods, and he entrusted similar sheets to Margul-Sperber and Corina. In assembling the volume *Der Sand aus den Urnen* he was to be forced to depend on his excellent memory, which had retained all of the poems. Paul Celan was never to see the manuscripts again.

In 1957, before her emigration from Romania, Ruth Lackner was to prepare a typescript of all the poems Celan had left with her—including those from the black calendar. This "Typescript 1957" was meant for Celan and was to be delivered to him as soon as Ruth was outside of Romania. But in those days the Romanian authorities had decreed a strict ban on the

Paul Celan

export of printed materials, and so the typescript remained in Bucharest until 1970. Then, because of a certain relaxation of the export regulations, it was taken out of Romania by friends of Ruth. Celan was notified, but before he was able to receive the typescript, he chose suicide.

The manuscripts left with Margul-Sperber came into other hands after his death in 1967 and were used for the unauthorized publications that appeared in Romania after 1970. From the same sources, single poems were said to have been published in the German Democratic Republic even during Celan's lifetime.

The most difficult parting before his departure from Bucharest was Celan's farewell to Ruth. Despite the easing of their relationship during the last years, his bond to her proved to be of great intensity for some time. In Ruth he saw a living symbol of the mother and the homeland. But Celan was to remain attached to his homeland for the remainder of his life. Even if, on the surface, the "wells" of the homeland seemed buried, in the depths a subterranean spring flowed along the "Meridian" that connected him with Czernowitz and the Bukovina.

Two poems from this time, "Das Ganze Leben" (The Whole Life) and "Harmonika" (Harmonica), most probably mark his farewell to Ruth. The following lines appear in the first one: "I whiled as a nightwind in your sister's venal lap. / Your hair hung in the tree above us, yet you were not there." And the second poem ends with: "More than you gave I dole out in the harbor as brandy. / Your hair remained spooled around the knife to me, your heart the smoking headland to us."[231]

With the help of Hungarian farmers, Paul crossed the Romanian-Hungarian border in 1947—the smuggling of people was well-organized and proceeded undisturbed. On the other side of the border he joined up with a group of Jewish emigrants and tried to make his way to Vienna. Since the trains were still running very erratically, they often had to stay nights in half-destroyed stations so as not to miss their next connection. But he considered the people with whom he was traveling as friends. They were Jews like him, and had suffered similar fates. In Celan's prose text "Conversation in the Mountains" a passage recalls these circumstances: "I lay on the stone, back then . . . on the stone tiles; and next to me, there they lay, the others who were like me . . . my cousins; . . . they did not love me and I did not love them, because I was one, and who wants to love one, and they were many. . ."[232]

By way of Budapest Paul finally reached Vienna, the object of his longing. But this city was to be a bitter disappointment to him. Although Celan had brought a letter of recommendation to Otto Basil[233] from Margul-Sperber and had within a few months established understanding friendships with Edgar Jené, Ingeborg Bachmann, Milo Dor, Reinhard Federmann, and Klaus Demus, life there was difficult. Ludwig von Ficker, a patron of Trakl and admirer of Celan's poetry, invited him to a lecture in Innsbruck, but was also unable to facilitate his stay in Vienna.

Celan maintained written correspondence with Ruth. On July 6, 1948, he wrote to her from Innsbruck:

> . . . Yesterday I was in Mühlau, in the churchyard where Trakl is buried. I had flowers with me . . . and on the way, in a meadow, I broke off a small twig which I laid on his grave from you. That evening I read poems at the home of Ludwig von Ficker, Trakl's friend. You can imagine how bashful I was. But Ludwig von Ficker then said to

me that I was eligible to come into the inheritance of
Else Lasker-Schüler. Else Lasker-Schüler is for the Fic-
kers, like Trakl, the embodiment of true poetry. She herself
was often in Mühlau, and one of her poetry cycles is
addressed to "Ludwig von Ficker, the Landvogt of Tyrolia
and his beautiful Swede." The "beautiful Swede," Ficker's
wife, is now an old Lady... She feels that I resemble
Else Lasker-Schüler—she said that to me before I even
read my poems, and that's how it remains in her mind
for all times... In about one week I am going to Paris...

On December 2, 1949, four days before her birthday, he
wrote to Ruth from Paris describing the past year as a "shadow
year and a dark year, which at least for me had no other name
than that of loneliness, seclusion, and reticence, and which
now wants to open up a little, so that the two birthday children
can give each other their best wishes.... Today's day is a
spring day, it is December-spring...."

And again on the occasion of Ruth's birthday, Paul Celan
wrote on December 2, 1951: "Wherever one went the world
was blooming. And yet despair gave birth to poetry."

"Auf Schritt und Tritt blühte die Welt. Und noch
aus den Verzweiflungen wurden Gedichte."

NOTES

Preface

1   Allemann, "Editorisches Nachwort," I, p. 421.
2   Hans-Georg Gadamer, *Wer bin Ich und wer bist Du? Ein Kommentar zu Paul Celans Gedichtfolge 'Atemkristall'* (Who Am I and Who Are You? A Commentary on Paul Celan's poetry sequence 'Breath-Crystal') (Frankfurt: Suhrkamp, 1973), p. 128.
3   Paul Celan, "Ansprache anlässlich der Entgegennahme des Literaturpreises der Freien Hansestadt Bremen" (Speech on the Occasion of Receiving the Literature Prize of the Free Hanseatic City of Bremen), 1958; and "Der Meridian. Rede anlässlich der Verleihung des Georg-Büchner-Preises" (The Meridian. Speech on the Occasion of Receiving the Georg Büchner Prize), Darmstadt 1960. Both in: Paul Celan, *Ausgewählte Gedichte. Zwei Reden.* Epilogue by Beda Allemann. (Frankfurt: Suhrkamp, 1968), pp. 125–129, 131–148. Also in: Paul Celan, *Collected Prose,* trans. Rosmarie Waldrop, (New York: Sheep Meadow Press, 1990).
4   "Die Wahrheit, die Laubfrösche, die Schriftsteller und die Klapperstörche," *34 * Erste Liebe. Dokumentarische Geschichten* (The Truth, the Tree-frogs, the Writers and the Storks. 34 * First Love. Documentary Stories), ed. Robert Neumann (Frankfurt: Bärmeier & Nikel, 1966), p. 32f.
5   Jerry Glenn, *Paul Celan* (New York: Twayne Publishers, 1973), p. 15.

I. The Unknown Landscape

6   Celan, "Bremer Ansprache," p. 127.
7   See Erich Beck, *Bukowina—Land zwischen Orient und Okzident* (Bukovina—Land Between Orient and Occident) (Freilassing: Pannonia, 1963).
The following additional sources were used for the history of the Bukovina and its Jews:
a)   *Geschichte der Juden in der Bukowina* (History of the Jews in the Bukovina), ed. Hugo Gold, 2 vols., (Tel Aviv: Olamenu, 1958 & 1963).
b)   Simon Dubnow, *Die neueste Geschichte des jüdischen Volkes* (The Most Recent History of the Jewish People) (Jerusalem: Hozaah Ivrith, 1938).
c)   Dubnow, Hebrew edition, Vol. 2, updated for the years 1936–1951 by S. L. Kirshenbaum (Tel Aviv: Dvir, 1956).

Notes

d)   Wolfgang von Waisel, "Juden in der österreichischen und österreichisch-
ungarischen Armee," (Jews in the Austrian and Austro-Hungarian Armies),
Zeitschrift für die Geschichte der Juden (Tel Aviv) 8 (1971), No. 1/2,
pp. 1–22.

8   Gold, Vol. 1, pp. 13, 16, 17, 22.
9   "Zaddik" (Hebrew for 'a righteous man') is the designation given to the leaders
of the Hasidic rabbinical dynasties.
10 Celan, "Bremer Ansprache," p. 127.
11 Celan, "Bremer Ansprache," p. 127.
12 Told by Léa Beaussier.
13 From "Oben, geräuschlos" *(Sprachgitter)* I, 188; Hamburger, p. 135.
14 Wilhelm Rosenblatt, "Czernowitz vor fünfzig Jahren" (Czernowitz Fifty Years
Ago), *Die Stimme* (Tel Aviv) 31 (Aug. 1975), No. 311, p. 7.
15 Leon Kellner (1859–1928) was appointed from Vienna in 1906 to Czernowitz
University, where he was active until 1918. In addition to his scientific and
professorial work, he also developed intensive social and political activities
within the Zionist Organization. He was the only university professor who made
his convictions publicly known. He became a member of the Bukovina's state
parliament and courageously represented the interests of the Jews. Kellner's
most important publications are:
a)   *Deutsch-Englisches und Englisch-Deutsches Handwörterbuch* (German-
English and English-German Dictionary) (Braunschweig: Vieweg & Sohn,
1902–1905).
b)   *Shakespeare-Wörterbuch* (Shakespeare Dictionary) (Leipzig: Tauchnitz,
1922).
c)   *Erläuterungen und Textverbesserungen zu 14 Dramen Shakespeares* (Commentary on and Textual Revisions of 14 Shakespearean Dramas) (Leipzig:
Tauchnitz, 1930, posthum.).
d)   *Meine Schüler. Mit einem Geleitwort von Richard Beer-Hofmann* (My Students. With a Preface by Richard Beer-Hofmann) (Vienna: Paul Zsolnay,
1930, posthum.).
On Kellner's biography:
Anna Kellner, *Leon Kellner. Sein Leben und Werk* (Leon Kellner. His Life and
his Work) (Vienna: Carl Geopolds Sohn, 1936).
16 The Toynbee Hall was named after the founder of similar institutions in England, who inspired Kellner. Arnold Toynbee (1852–1883), the English academic
and social reformer, considered it his mission to "find and help the workers and
the poor."
17 Letter from Paul Celan to Gideon Kraft, 7 May 1968.

II. Speak My Name

18 Information on the history of Celan's family and the circumstances of his birth

Notes

was provided by his close relatives: his father's sisters, Berta Antschel (letter) and Minna Brettschneider (conversation and letter); his mother's sister, Blanca Berman (conversation); Celan's cousin Edith Hubermann, daughter of Regina Rones, his father's sister (conversation); his mother's stepbrother, Esriel Schrager (conversation and letters). In addition, Ovadia Singer, an early friend of Celan's father, told of his father's school days in Czernowitz and of his choice of profession. This report was passed on to the author by Gideon Kraft. Regina Rones, Celan's father's sister, was present during a conversation with family members, but only participated by nodding approvingly in response to commentary by the others.

19 See II Moses 12, 13.
20 Told by Ruth Lackner. The quote is from "Beim Hagelkorn" (By the Hailstone) *(Atemwende)* II, 22.
21 From "Es ist alles anders" (Everything's Different) *(Die Niemandsrose)* I, 285.
22 "Eine Gauner-und Ganovenweise" *(Die Niemandsrose)* I, 229f.
23 From "Es ist alles anders."
24 Conversation with Emma Lustig.
25 The quote was reported by Ruth Lackner.
26 From "So bist du denn geworden" (That's what you have become) *(Mohn und Gedächtnis)* I, 59.

III. Near You One Is Cramped

27 Conversation with Emma Lustig. Emma Lustig and her sister, Klara Lindenfeld, both née Nagel, Celan's paternal cousins once removed, told the author in a joint conversation about Celan's childhood (in addition to those relatives mentioned in footnote 18). The students of the lower Gymnasium level were described by Celan's high school colleagues Sieghard ("Harry") Alper (conversation), Gustav Chomed (first conversation), Israel Hochstätt (conversation), and Yancu Pesate (letters).
28 Conversation with Emma Lustig and Klara Lindenfeld.
29 Conversation with Klara Lindenfeld.
30 "Drüben" (Over There), *Der Sand aus den Urnen*, p. 5.
31 Conversation with Emma Lustig.
32 Conversation with Etka Frankowitz, a former colleague of Celan's at the Meisler school. See also Rosa Hoffer, "Die Meisler-Schule" (The Meisler School), *Die Stimme* (Tel Aviv) 34 (May 1978), No. 339. The former French teacher at the school mentions in the article that Celan attended this institution.
33 For a long time it was impossible to verify whether Celan had in fact attended the Safah-Ivriah Hebrew school. In 1971 Edith Hubermann mentioned this school as the most probable one for Paul at this stage, but she herself was not certain. His other relatives did not remember anything about it. School friends of Celan's from the Gymnasium were also unable to furnish more precise information. It was not until 1973 that Etka Frankowitz, a former student at

195

Notes

the Meisler school, was able to state unequivocally that Celan was in her class only in the first grade. She did not know where he continued his schooling. Then, in 1975, Yancu Pesate confirmed that Celan most likely had been a student at the Hebrew school, since he himself had attended the Meisler school for four years without having Celan as a classmate. He did not meet him until in the Gymnasium. The final proof that Celan attended the Hebrew school from the second to the fourth grade (that is, up to his entrance in the Gymnasium) came from his former classmate, Mia Schmul, who spoke to the author in the spring of 1977. She also owns a photograph of the graduating class at Safah-Ivriah.

34 Told by Esriel Schrager. See also Celan's poem, "Hawdalah" (Havdala) (*Die Niemandsrose*) I, 259, which evokes the observance of the closing of the Sabbath.

35 Arnold Daghani, *Lasst mich leben!* (Let me Live!) (Tel Aviv: Weg und Ziel, 1960), p. 48. The book was prefaced and translated from English ("The Grave is in the Cherry Orchard," *Adam* (London) 1946) by Siegfried Rosenzweig. Daghani's personal recollection of the young poetess and her gruesome death were passed on to the author by Hersh Segal.

36 The excerpt from "Poem" is quoted from a private printing of poems that Hersh Segal, at one point her teacher in Czernowitz, collected, and for which he wrote an epilogue: Selma Meerbaum-Eisinger (1924–1942), *Blütenlese. Gedichte* (Flower Harvest. Poems) (Israel: Rechovot, 1976), p. 32. Also in German (Hamburg: Hoffmann und Campe, 1980); and in *Ich bin in Sehnsucht eingehüllt* (I am Shrouded in Longing), (Frankfurt: Fischer, 1990). This volume contains all the poems from the manuscript found with Selma Meerbaum's friends after the war. "Poem" appeared in slightly shortened form as early as 1968 in the anthology edited by Heinz Seydel: *Welch Wort in die Kälte gerufen. Die Judenverfolgungen des Dritten Reiches im deutschen Gedicht* (Which Word Shouted into the Cold. The Third Reich's Persecution of Jews in German Poetry) (Berlin, GDR: Verlag der Nation, 1968), p. 352. The main reason why Paul Celan agreed to include his poem "Death Fugue" in this volume was to present the poem as a memorial to his relative, Selma Meerbaum. In 1969 he made a gift of this volume to his childhood friend David Seidmann and pointed out to him the poem, "Poem."

37 Conversation with Emma Lustig and Klara Lindenfeld.

38 Letter from Berta Antschel.

39 Conversation with Sieghard Alper.

40 Letter from Paul Schafler. The two Pauls were related through their grandmothers, who were sisters (in Paul Antschel's paternal and Paul Schafler's maternal lines). Both Pauls also shared the first name of their common ancestor, Pessach Antschel (reported in a letter from Edith Hubermann).

41 "Hutsuls" are the native horses of northern Bukovina, named after the peasants who inhabit the area.

42 Letter from Paul Schafler.

43 Conversations with Dorothea Müller-Altneu and Emma Lustig.

Notes

44 Letter from Paul Schafler.
45 Eliezer Steinbarg, *Mesholim* (Fables) (Czernowitz: Verlag des Jiddischen Schulvereins, 1932); later (Tel Aviv: I. L. Peretz, 1969), p. 70. Steinbarg (1890–1932) was born in Bessarabia, but lived in Czernowitz after 1919. Through his "fables" he became well-known in Yiddish-speaking Eastern Europe and in America. He also published books of fairy tales and children's plays, and he translated modern Hebrew literature into Yiddish. The bulk of his work remains unpublished.
46 Conversation with Ilana Schmueli.
47 Conversation with Edith Hubermann.

IV. Growth

48 Conversation with Yitzhak Alpan.
49 Conversation with Esriel Schrager.
50 Letter from Joachim Bittmann.
51 From "Oben, geräuschlos" (Above, soundless) (*Sprachgitter*) I, 188; "Le Menhir" (*Die Niemandsrose*) I, 260; "Königswut" (*Atemwende*) II, 81; the latter also in Hamburger, p. 225.
52 This letter is in the possession of the addressee, Minna Brettschneider, who kindly made it available to the author. The italicized words are underlined in the original; "Donia" is the diminutive form of David, the name of Aunt Minna's husband; the awkward English quote clearly shows that Celan had at this stage not yet begun to learn this language.
53 Conversation with Yitzhak Alpan.
54 Conversation with Sieghard Alper.
55 Conversations with Manuel Singer.
56 Conversations with Gustav Chomed.
57 Conversation with Ernst Engler.
58 Second conversation with Gustav Chomed.
59 See the remarks in the next chapter, which are also connected with the beginning of Celan's poetic creations.

V. There Was a Freedom

60 Paul's time at school was described in conversations by Yitzhak Alpan, Israel Hochstätt, Manuel Singer, and in letters by Yancu Pesate.
61 Conversations with Manuel Singer.
62 Conversations with Manuel Singer. Sieghard Alper reported that even in the lower Gymnasium grades another Romanian professor was impressed with Celan's wide reading in and good pronunciation of the Romanian language.
63 Conversation with Israel Hochstätt.

Notes

64 Second letter from Yancu Pesate.
65 Conversations with Minna Brettschneider, Esriel Schrager, and Manuel Singer.
66 Conversation with Israel Hochstätt.
67 Told by Ruth Lackner, who emphasized, however, that she knew Leo Antschel had in fact been a perfectly respectable man. This judgment was confirmed by Ilse Goldmann, who speaks in her letter of Celan's "upright" father of "limited intelligence."
68 Conversations with Israel Hochstätt and Jacob Silbermann. Also the oral report by Ovadia Singer, as reported by Gideon Kraft.
69 Letter from Ilse Goldmann, who also writes, "How is Paul's upright, limited father to understand what a strange gift fate had given him."
70 Conversation with Sieghard Alper.
71 Conversation with Leonid Miller.
72 Conversation with Israel Hochstätt. All those interviewed by the author, with the exception of Ernst Engler, knew of Paul's participation in the anti-fascist youth group. Ilse Goldmann, Erika Yeshayahu, Lola Graur, and Ruth Kaswan also spoke of this.
73 Letter from Ilse Goldmann.
74 Conversation with Israel Hochstätt. For the parody see Rilke's poem "Ernste Stunde" (Serious Hour) in *The Book of Images*, Vol. 1, Pt. 2.
75 Letter from Ilse Goldmann.
76 Letter from Ilse Goldmann.
77 Conversations with Gustav Chomed, Jacob Silbermann, and Ruth Lackner.
78 Told by Ruth Lackner.
79 Conversation with Ruth Tal.
80 With "we" Ruth Kaswan here means herself and her closest friend at the time, Edith (Silbermann-)Horowitz.
81 Ruth Kaswan's letter also includes the sentence, "But we did not deem Baudelaire particularly important, at least not at that time."
82 Letter from Ruth Kaswan.
83 Conversations with Erika Yeshayahu, Melitta Steiner, and Malzia Fischmann-Kahwe; letters from Lola Graur, Pearl Fichmann, and Ruth Kaswan.
84 Conversation with Ernst Engler.
85 Rainer Maria Rilke, "Die Aufzeichnungen des Malte Laurids Brigge," *Sämtliche Werke* ed. Rilke Archives with Ruth Sieber-Rilke, Ernst Zinn, (Frankfurt: Insel, 1966), Vol. 6, p. 777. Also in English, *The Notebooks of Malte Laurids Brigge*, trans. Stephen Mitchell (New York: Vintage, 1985).
86 Dorothea Müller-Altneu, speech on the occasion of a Celan commemoration, Haifa, 22 July 1970; with the kind permission of the speaker.
87 Letter from Ilse Goldmann.
88 Conversations with Esriel Schrager and Malzia Fischmann-Kahwe.
89 Conversations with Yitzhak Alpan and Ruth Tal; letter from Siegried Trichter.
90 Conversation with Yitzhak Alpan, Gustav Chomed, and Manuel Singer. Ruth Lackner spoke of Celan's refusal to show Weissglas his poems.

Notes

91 Conversations with Ruth Lackner. None of Celan's early male friends who have been interviewed can remember having heard conversations about poetry in general or Celan's poetry in particular.
92 Conversation with Yitzhak Alpan.
93 For more on these collections, see Chapter 10.
94 "Klage," TS 44. "Kein ankerloses Tasten stört die Hand" and "Die Mutter, lautlos heilend," MS 44/45; the first of the two appears with the Mother's Day comment in TS 44. "Heimkehr" is in both typescripts, but is dated only in TS 57. "Während der Reise" is found in TS 57 and, under the title "Landschaft" (Landscape), without comment, also in TS 44.
95 The notebook is in possession of Ruth Lackner.
96 Dorothea Müller-Altneu, "Unser Paul" (Our Paul), *Die Stimme* (Tel Aviv) 26 (July 1970), No. 245, p. 6. Also conversation with Ilana Schmueli.
97 Conversation with Israel Hochstätt.
98 Conversations with Manuel Singer.
99 The high school diploma (Abiturzeugnis) is in the possession of Gisèle Celan-Lestrange, who was kind enough to let the author see it.
100 Letter from Ilse Goldmann and conversations with Ruth Lackner.
101 Conversation with Esriel Schrager.
102 Conversations with Manuel Singer.
103 Conversation with Yitzhak Alpan.
104 From "Landschaft," or "Während der Reise," see note 94. The fact that this poem was not included in MS 44/45 could indicate that Celan no longer considered the poem as valuable, for the style of his poetry had already changed by the end of 1944.
105 Ludwig Strauss, *Jüdische Volkslieder* (Jewish Folk Songs) (Berlin: Schocken, 1935), p. 21.
106 "La Contrescarpe" *(Die Niemandsrose)* I, 283.
107 Conversations with Manuel Singer and letter from Berta Antschel.

VI. Memory of France

108 It was clearly no coincidence that Celan, upon moving to Paris after the war, again decided to live in the rue de l'Ecole. The time Celan spent in Tours is described in letters and conversations by Eliyahu Pinter, Berta Antschel, Yitzhak Alpan, Gustav Chomed, Ilse Goldmann, Leonid Miller, Manuel Singer, and Yancu Pesate.
109 See Maurice Nadeau, *Histoire du Surréalisme* (History of Surrealism) (Paris: Editions du Seuil, 1945).
110 See "In eins" (In One) *(Die Niemandsrose)* I, 270. The Hebrew name "Abadias" (Obadja) means "servant of God."

Notes

VII. Cyrillics

111 After studying abroad for many years, the author lived in Czernowitz again after the autumn of 1939. The description of events at this time are based on his own observations. On November 1, 1941, he was deported to Transnistria. After the liberation in March 1944, he did not return to his native city, but emigrated via Romania to Palestine.

112 Letter from Chaim Ginniger. Gurahumora is a popular vacation spot in the Bukovina Carpathian mountains.

113 Müller-Altneu, "Unser Paul," p. 6.

114 Letter from Paul Celan to Gideon Kraft, 23 April 1968, in which the latter first proposed inviting Celan to Israel. As a result, the cultural section of the Histadrut (Labor Union), over which Jehuda Eren-Ehrenkranz was presiding at the time, invited Celan to Israel. The visit did not take place, however, until November 1969.

115 Conversations with Ruth Lackner, Sieghard Alper, and Malzia Fischmann-Kahwe.

116 Müller-Altneu, speech.

117 Conversation with Yitzhak Alpan; italicized words correspond to Alper's emphases.

118 Conversation with Ilana Schmueli.

119 Müller-Altneu, speech.

120 Müller-Altneu, speech.

121 Conversations with David Seidmann, Erika Yeshayahu, and Dorothea Müller-Altneu. Also Müller-Altneu, "Unser Paul."

122 Conversation with David Seidmann.

123 Conversations with Ruth Lackner.

124 Müller-Altneu, speech.

125 Müller-Altneu, "Unser Paul."

126 Conversations with Gustav Chomed.

127 "Dunstbänder-, Spruchbänder-Aufstand" (Atemwende) II, 102; Hamburger, p. 269.

VIII. The Glow of Berenice's Hair

128 This chapter is mainly based on conversations with Ruth Lackner and the extensive correspondence the author exchanged with her over the years. Quotations from written reports of conversations or from the letters are presented in quotes; other sources are noted separately.

129 Conversation with Dorothea Müller-Altneu.

130 Conversations with Ruth Lackner.

130a See "Bergfrühling," Der Sand aus den Urnen, p. 12.

131 "Sindbad" and "Die Schneekönigin," MS 44/45. "Sindbad" also in TS 44.

Notes

132 Steinbarg, *Mesholim*, p. 46f.

133 The Yiddish poet Itzik Manger (1901–1969), born in Czernowitz to a master tailor, belonged in the 1920s to the "Yiddish Schools Association," a group founded by Eliezer Steinbarg. In the 1930s he lived first in Romania, later in Poland. His first book of poetry "Stern oifn Dach" (Star on the Roof) appeared in Bucharest in 1929. Later, he published three more volumes of Yiddish poetry in Warsaw and, in 1939, the novel *Das Buch vom Paradis*, trans. Salcia Landmann, (Geneva/Hamburg: Kossodo, 1963); in English, *The Book of Paradise: The Wonderful Adventures of Shmuel-Aba Abervo*, trans. Leonard Wolf, (New York: Hill and Wang, 1965). During the Second World War, he lived in London and New York, where two volumes of "collected poems" were published. Manger died shortly after his emigration to Israel, where he had found extensive recognition.

134 Hersh Segal told of the friendship between Celan, Lewin, and himself, and in many other conversations about his memories of Celan. In Czernowitz in 1934, Segal (b. 1905), Chaim Ginniger and others published the "Klejne Antologie" "Naje Jidiśe Dichtung" (Small Anthology—New Yiddish Poetry), a novel project in that the Yiddish texts were printed in the Latin instead of the usual Hebraic alphabet. Segal printed a similar anthology of German-Jewish poetry from the Bukovina with Alfred Kittner. He also collected and published in Czernowitz many portfolios of Jewish painters and sketch artists, which attracted the attention of art lovers. The last collection he was able to publish in Czernowitz were the *Lider mit Nigunim* (Song Melodies) (app. 1939) of the Yiddish poet Selik Berditschewer, the bard of Yiddish folk art.

135 "Les Adieux," TS 44 and MS 44/45.

136 See Rilke's "Requiem," *The Book of Images*, Vol. 2, Pt. 2. Also Celan's "Edgar Jené und der Traum vom Traume" (Edgar Jené and the Dream About the Dream) (Vienna: Agathon, 1948); in English in Waldrop. Celan's text was reprinted in *Die Pestsäule* (Vienna) 1 (1972/73), No. 1, pp. 22–25.

137 Both appear in TS 44 and MS 44/45. "Schlaflied" is not to be confused with a poem of the same name in *Der Sand aus den Urnen* (p. 7), which appeared in MS 44/45 as "Das andere Schlaflied" (The Other Lullaby).

138 The five quotations are from the following five poems, which all appeared in MS 44/45, the first four also in TS 44: "Mein Karren knarrt nicht mehr" (My carriage no longer creaks) (untitled), "Rosenschimmer" (Glimmer of Roses), "Herbst" (Autumn), "Lautlose, Liebliche, Leichte" (Noiseless, lovely, light one) (untitled), "Der Tage Trost" (The Days' Consolation).

139 From "Prinzessin Nimmermüd" (Princess Tireless), TS 44 and MS 44/45.

140 The quotations are from the following six poems: "Wandlung" (Transformation), TS 44 and MS 44/45; "Mohn" (Poppy), MS 44/45, in TS 44 untitled, beginning with the line "Die Nacht mit fremden Feuern zu versehen" (To provide the night with alien fires), later in *Der Sand aus den Urnen*, p. 11; "Tulpen" (Tulips), MS 44/45, in TS 44 untitled, "Tulpen, ein stummes Gestirn" (Tulips, silent stars); "Windröschen" (Anemones), MS 44/45, in TS 44 as "Anemone

Notes

nemorosa"; "Mein Karren knarrt nicht mehr," TS 44 and MS 44/45; "Beisammen" (Together), TS 57.

141 "Sternenlied," MS 44/45.

142 From "Aus der Tiefe" (Out of the Depths), MS 44/45.

143 The eight quotations are from the following poems: "Die Nacht, die die Stirnen uns mass" (The night that measured our brows), untitled, first and seventh quotes; "Stundenwechsel" (Change of Hours), second, third, and fourth quotes; "Mystisches Lied" (Mystical Song), fifth and sixth quotes; "Sindbad," eighth quote. All the poems, with the exception of the first, which only appears in TS 57, are found in both TS 44 and MS 44/45. The poem "Mystisches Lied" was published under the title "Schwarze Krone" (Black Crown) in *Die Tat* (Zurich) 7 Feb. 1948.

144 Conversation with Stella Avni.

145 "Finsternis," "Erinnerung," "Beieinander," and "Ich weiss vom Fels," in both TS 44 and MS 44/45.

146 The first quote forms the ending of the poem "Zur Laute" (To the Lute), MS 44/45, the quote also appears in TS 44 at the end of an untitled poem, "Schwarz / legt nun der einsame den Finger" (Black, / the lonely one now lays his finger); the second quotation is the beginning of an untitled poem from MS 44/45, in TS 44 it is still titled "Ich lass dich" (I let you).

147 "Schlaflosigkeit," TS 44, MS 44/45.

148 "Legende," TS 44, TS 57.

149 "Dornenkranz" and "Taglied," TS 44, MS 44/45.

150 "Seidelbast," MS 44/45, in TS 44 untitled, "Von diesen Stauden."

151 "Es regnet, Schwester," untitled, TS 44 and MS 44/45; also in *Der Sand aus den Urnen*, p. 9, under the title, "Regenflieder" (Rain-lilacs).

IX. Towards the Abyss

152 Gold, Vol. 2, pp. 13, 44f.

153 Conversations with Ruth Lackner, Gustav Chomed, and Malzia Fischmann-Kahwe.

154 From written reports of conversations with Leonid Miller and Yitzhak Alpan. Additional information about Erich Einhorn came from Paula Einhorn, Kurt Einhorn, and Malzia Fischmann-Kahwe. Einhorn (1920–1974) was a Russian soldier during the War. After the conquest of Vienna and Berlin, he worked in both cities as an interpreter. He married a Russian woman and lived in Moscow after the war, editing German-language newspapers and translating from Russian. Paul Celan renewed their friendship in 1962. Although Einhorn could not receive mail directly, Paul was able to send him letters with the help of Gustav Chomed, who had returned to Soviet Czernowitz. According to his former colleague in Moscow, Jenny Fratkina, Erich felt frustrated during the last years of his life. His cousin, Dori Evian, who was able to correspond with

Notes

Erich a few months before his death, told the author that Erich's letters had been "full of melancholy." Erich Einhorn died from a sudden heart attack before he was able to answer a letter from the author.

155 "Schibboleth" *(Von Schwelle zu Schwelle)* I, 132; Hamburger, p. 97. The author is indebted to Dorothea Müller-Altneu for pointing out the meaning of the name "Einhorn."

156 Gold, Vol. 2, pp. 11, 49ff., 70ff.

157 Reports about Paul's time in forced labor came from Ruth Lackner, David Seidmann, and Dorothea Müller-Altneu.

158 Told by David Seidmann.

159 Told by Ruth Lackner.

160 From "Das ausgeschachtete Herz" (The Excavated Heart) *(Fadensonnen)* II, 150.

161 Reports about life in the camps came from Oswald Weidler and David Seidmann, who were in the same camp as Paul.

162 "Festland," TS 44 and MS 44/45; also published, with the help of Max Rychner, in *Die Tat* (Zurich), 7 Feb. 1948.

163 Information about the deportees of 1942 is from:
   a) *Encyclopedia of Jewish Communities, Rumania I* (Jerusalem: Yad Vashem, 1969); in Hebrew.
   b) Daghani (see note 35).
   c) Peter Duhr, *Inferno* (Berlin: Rütten & Loening, 1956).

164 "Engführung," *(Sprachgitter)* I, 197f.

165 *Encyclopedia*, p. 496. Gold (Vol. 2, p. 75) also mentions that a Jewish violinist was ordered to play music for the "orgies."

166 The disease caused by chick peas (Lathyrism) was studied in Transnistria by the physician Arthur Kessler. He reported on it in the *Monatsschrift für Psychiatrie und Neurologie* (Basel) Vol. 113 (1947), No. 6, pp. 1–32. In the conclusion he writes, "Many of the sick wound up . . . badly crippled."

167 *Encyclopedia*, p. 496, trans. from Hebrew by the author.

168 Daghani, p. 27. In addition, the author was told by Hersh Segal that Daghani was certain that Leo Antschel did not return from Gaisin and that his execution by the SS was publicly known in the fall of 1942.

169 "Schwarze Flocken," *Der Sand aus den Urnen*, p. 19. Also untitled in TS 57.

170 "Grabschrift für François" *(Von Schwelle zu Schwelle)*, I, 105; "Vor einer Kerze," 110f.; "Andenken," 121. In his book on Paul Celan (p. 49) Jerry Glenn fails to mention this poem when he asserts that "Schwarze Flocken" is the only poem in which Celan was thinking of his father.

171 "Mit wechselndem Schlüssel" *(Von Schwelle zu Schwelle)* I, 112.

172 From "Winter," TS 44, MS 44/45; untitled in TS 57, "Es fällt nun, Mutter, Schnee in der Ukraine" (Snow is falling, Mother, in the Ukraine). It was also published untitled by Alfred Kittner, who does not know MS 44/45, in *Neue Literatur* (Bucharest) 21 (1970), No. 5.

173 Benno Teitler, Paul's cousin once removed, who was able to escape from the

Notes

camp on the Bug, was the first to bring the news of Celan's mother's death to Czernowitz.

174 From "Gesang zur Sonnenwende" (Song to the Solstice), TS 57 and *Der Sand aus den Urnen*, p. 43.

175 "Ein Rosenkelch," TS 57. The first letters of each line in this acrostic poem combine to spell "Ruth Geliebte" (Beloved Ruth).

176 From "Königschwarz" (King's Black), TS 57. The metaphor of the "king" in connection with Judaism appears more frequently in Celan's later poetry.

177 "Das Fenster im Südturm," MS 44/45. Ruth Lackner also owns the piece of paper on which Celan first wrote the poem.

178 "Herbst" is contained in the notebook owned by Ruth Lackner. A different poem appears under the same title in TS 44 and MS 44/45.

179 Conversation with Stella Avni.

180 Conversations with Ruth Lackner.

181 From the written report of a conversation with Rose Ausländer. The author is much indebted to Rose Ausländer for this conversation, conducted in May 1972. Rose Ausländer (1907–1988) published her first book of poems, *Der Regenbogen* (The Rainbow), in 1939 in Czernowitz. After suffering from the persecutions of the Second World War, she emigrated to the United States in 1946 and began to write and publish poetry in English. In 1965 (after she had moved to Düsseldorf) her second collection of poetry appeared, *Blinder Sommer* (Blind Summer), followed by a series of further volumes in German: *36 Gerechte* (36 Just Ones) 1967, *Inventar* (Inventory) 1972, *Ohne Visum* (Without a Visa) and *Andere Zeichen* (Other Signs) 1974, *Gesammelte Gedichte* (Collected Poems) and *Noch ist Raum* (There's Still Room) 1976, *Doppelspiel* (Doubles) 1977.

182 Told by Jacob Silbermann.

183 "Ein Lied in der Wüste," *Der Sand aus den Urnen*, p. 25; "Die letzte Fahne," p. 41. Both also in *(Mohn und Gedächtnis)* I, 11, 23.

184 Told by Jacob Silbermann.

X. Alien Homeland

185 "Russischer Frühling," MS 44/45; also published by Alfred Kittner in *Neue Literatur* (Bucharest) 21 (1970), No. 5.

186 Letter from Konrad Deligdisch. Deligdisch had met Paul in the anti-fascist youth group, but he emphasizes that he was never "friends with" Paul. In fact, it is said that they never even exchanged personal words, because Paul was "shy" and Deligdisch himself "arrogant." In his eyes, Paul belonged at the time to the "decadent bourgeoisie."

187 For more on the Czechoslovak Legion in the Bukovina, see Michael Stepanek, "Sadagura-Cernovice-Prag," *Die Stimme* (Tel Aviv) 31 (May 1975), No. 303.

188 Told by Hersh Segal.

189 Conversations with Ruth Lackner.

Notes

190 Alfred Kittner, (1906–1991), was a journalist and in 1938 published his first book of poems in Czernowitz, *Der Wolkenreiter* (The Cloud Rider). After the war, he worked in Bucharest at the Romanian broadcasting organization. Later he dedicated himself entirely to a literary career, working on the *Neue Literatur*, the German-language publication of the Romanian Writers' Union. Notable in this context is his publication of German "Poems from the Bukovina," *Neue Literatur* 22 (1971), Nos. 11, 12.

Immanuel Weissglas, (1920–1979), did not become known as a German-Romanian poet in Bucharest until after the war. His first volume of poetry, *Kariera am Bug* (Quarry on the Bug) appeared there in 1947. Like Kittner, he contributed to *Neue Literatur*. In 1972 Kriterion published his collection of poems under the title *Der Nobiskrug* (according to Weissglas, the Nobiskrug is, following German legend, the final resting place for souls before their passage into the Beyond), in which his early poems are supplemented by newer ones.

191 From the written report of the conversation with Rose Ausländer.

192 Conversation with Dorothea Müller-Altneu.

193 Müller-Altneu, speech.

194 Müller-Altneu, speech.

195 Conversation with David Seidmann.

196 Conversations with Ruth Lackner.

197 "Flügelrauschen," *Der Sand aus den Urnen*, p. 17, also in TS 57 untitled, "Die Taube aber säumt in Avalun" (Yet the dove tarries in Avalon). "Der Pfeil der Artemis," *Der Sand aus den Urnen*, p. 15; also in MS 44/45 untitled and dedicated to Alfred Margul-Sperber, "Die Zeit tritt ehern in ihr letztes Alter" (Time brazenly enters its last age).

198 See Celan's letters to Ruth Lackner in chapter 9.

199 One copy of the carefully wire-bound TS 44 is in the possession of Hersh Segal, another with Jacob Silbermann, and Celan's copy probably remained in Bucharest.

200 Alfred Margul-Sperber, *Gleichnisse der Landschaft* (Landscape Allegories) (Storojineți: privately printed, 1934). Margul-Sperber (1898–1967) lived for several years in Vienna, Paris, and in the United States. He established many literary connections—among others, Otto Basil in Vienna and Max Rychner in Zurich—which remained intact through correspondence until the Second World War. In 1936 Sperber met the Austrian poet Josef Weinheber in Vienna and was very impressed with him. In 1939 Sperber published his second volume of poetry, *Geheimnis und Verzicht* (Mystery and Sacrifice), in the Czernowitz publishing house "Literaria." It is dedicated to the "Lords of Flondor," for whom Sperber worked for many years as an accountant in the management of their manor. After the war, he lived in Bucharest, where he contributed to German-language publications and published further books of poetry. In 1975 Alfred Kittner organized the posthumous publication of a selection of Sperber's collected works under the title of the second poetry volume, *Geheimnis und Verzicht* (Bucharest: Kriterion).

Notes

201 Celan, "Bremer Ansprache," p. 127.

202 From the written reports of conversations with Ruth Lackner.

203 Conversation with Malzia Fischmann-Kahwe.

204 Letter from Celan to Tanja Sternberg, 1 Jan. 1962.

205 Letter from Celan to Gideon Kraft, 7 May 1968.

206 See "Blume" (Flower) (*Sprachgitter*) I, 164.

207 Conversations with Ruth Lackner.

208 The pseudonym was not dropped until the third edition of *The Peasants*, in 1949. The translator then appeared as Paul Ancel.

209 Ruth Lackner and Leonid Miller provided information on the activities of the Bucharest publishing house.

210 Conversations with Ruth Lackner.

211 "Das Gastmahl," TS 57; *Der Sand aus den Urnen*, p. 44; (*Mohn und Gedächtnis*) I, 25. "Ein wasserfarbenes Wild," *Der Sand aus den Urnen*, p. 41; (*Mohn und Gedächtnis*) I, 23, under the title "Die letzte Fahne." "Das Geheimnis der Farne," MS 44/45; *Der Sand aus den Urnen*, p. 38; (*Mohn und Gedächtnis*) I, 21. The publication *Agora* was initially conceived as a periodical. However, its publication was financed by the Royal-Romanian cultural foundation, which ceased to exist after the Romanian king was forced to abdicate and leave the country. Thus only one issue of *Agora* appeared.

212 Conversation with Jacob Silbermann, who reported that he had helped Celan find the poetic pseudonym 'Celan' shortly before the latter left the city of his birth for good.

213 Letter from Petre Solomon.

214 Petre Solomon has so far published four poems and a short lyrical prose text, which Celan had written in Romanian: *Viaţa Româneasca* (Bucharest) 13 (1970), No. 7, p. 53f.; *Secolul* (Bucharest) 20 (1971), No. 1-2-3, p. 79f. In 1976 he announced his intention to publish other texts (poems, prose, and translations of Kafka's work), which Celan wrote in Bucharest in Romanian (letter from Solomon to Ruth Lackner, 29 March 1976).

215 Conversations with Ruth Lackner.

216 From Celan, "Antwort auf die Enquête 'Le Problème du Bilinguisme'" *Almanach 1961 de la Librairie Flinker* (Paris). English: "Reply to a Questionnaire from the Flinker Bookstore, Paris, 1961," Waldrop.

217 Petre Solomon, "Amintiri despre Paul Celan" (Memories of Paul Celan), *Viaţa Româneasca* (Bucharest) 13 (1970), No. 7, pp. 47–52. The quotation, translated from Romanian by the author, appears with Solomon's kind permission. "The 'evening booklet' remained only a project," writes Solomon in his letter to the author.

218 Nina Cassian and Petre Solomon translated a selection of Celan's work into Romanian and published it: Paul Celan, *Versuri* (Verses) (Bucharest: Editura Univers, 1973). Celan's relations with people in the literary circles of Bucharest was described to the author in a conversation with Yitzhak Gorenstein.

219 Janos Szasz: " 'Es ist nicht so einfach . . .' Erinnerungen an Paul Celan; Seiten

Notes

aus einem amerikanischen Tagebuch" ('It's not so easy . . .' Memories of Paul Celan; Pages from an American Diary), *Neue Literatur* (Bucharest) 26 (1976), No. 11, p. 32.

220 Conversation with Leonid Miller.

221 For more on Ghérasim Luca and his colleagues in Bucharest see: Jean-Louis Bédouin, *La poésie surréaliste* (Surrealist Poetry) (Paris: Seghers, 1964).

222 The surrealist poet Paul Păun is the physician Dr. Zaharia Zaharia, who told the author about the Bucharest surrealists in a conversation.

223 Comment by Ovid Crohmălniceanu, passed on by Janos Szasz (see note 219).

224 Conversation with Malzia Fischmann-Kahwe.

225 "Coagula," *(Atemwende)* II, 83. The author thanks Ruth Lackner for pointing out this connection, which appears to agree with the opinions of Celan's other early friends.

226 Told by Ruth Lackner.

227 Zaharia Zaharia (Paul Păun) wrote to the author: "In 1947 it was our joint project—along with D. Trost and Ghérasim Luca—to find a way across the border. I don't know why [Celan] undertook this adventure on his own. But I am glad that it worked out well for him, for he succeeded where we did not." (Translated from Romanian by the author).

228 Report from Arnold Daghani, for which the author is indebted to Hersh Segal.

229 Conversation with Leonid Miller.

230 Conversations with Ruth Lackner.

231 "Das ganze Leben" and "Harmonika" were among the poems written on loose sheets of paper that were later compiled into TS 57. Also in *Der Sand aus den Urnen*, p. 51, 28; "Das ganze Leben" also in *(Mohn und Gedächtnis)* I, 34.

232 Paul Celan, "Gespräch im Gebirg" (Conversation in the Mountains) *Neue Rundschau* 71 (1960), No. 2, pp. 199–202. In English in Waldrop.

233 Excerpts from the letter of recommendation from Alfred Margul-Sperber were published by Otto Basil in the last issue of *Plan* (Vienna) 2 (spring 1948), No. 6, p. 423. The same issue also included seventeen of Celan's previously unpublished poems. These excerpts were reprinted in an essay by Milo Dor, "Paul Celan" in *Über Paul Celan* (On Paul Celan), ed. Dietlind Meinecke (Frankfurt: Suhrkamp, 1970), 2nd expanded Ed., p. 282. Margul-Sperber also sent several Celan poems to Max Rychner in Zurich, who published them in *Die Tat* (Zurich), 7 Feb. 1948.

INDEXES

INDEX OF SOURCES

Index of persons who provided information on Celan's youth. The codes, *L*, for letter and *C*, for conversation, are followed by their respective dates. *O* indicates those who were helpful in providing additional sources.

INDEX OF NAMES

(italics refer to notes)

Indexes

211

Indexes

Indexes

Indexes